REBIRTH

REBIRTH

Political, Economic, and
Social Development in First Nations

edited by

ANNE-MARIE MAWHINEY

Dundurn Press
Toronto & Oxford

Editor: John Parry
Printed and bound in Canada by WEBCOM, Scarborough, Ontario

The publisher wishes to acknowledge the generous assistance and ongoing support of **The Canada Council, The Book Publishing Industry Development Program** of the **Department of Communications, The Ontario Arts Council, The Ontario Publishing Centre** of the **Ministry of Culture, Tourism and Recreation,** and **The Ontario Heritage Foundation.**
     Care has been taken to trace the ownership of copyright material used in the text (including the illustrations). The author and publisher welcome any information enabling them to rectify any reference or credit in subsequent editions.

J. Kirk Howard, Publisher

Canadian Cataloguing in Publication Data

Main entry under title:

Rebirth : political, economic and social development in First Nations

Proceedings of the 3rd annual conference of the
Institute of Northern Ontario Research and Development
held in 1992 at Laurentian University.
Includes bibliographical references.
ISBN 1-55002-194-X

1. Indians of North America. – Ontario – Congresses.
I. Mawhiney, Anne-Marie, 1953–   . II. Laurentian
University of Sudbury. Institute of Northern
Ontario Research and Development. Conference
(3rd : 1992 : Laurentian University).

E78.05R4   1993   971.3'00497   C93-095512-9

Dundurn Press Limited
2181 Queen Street East
Suite 301
Toronto, Canada
M4E 1E5

Dundurn Distribution
73 Lime Walk
Headington, Oxford
England
OX3 7AD

Dundurn Press Limited
1823 Maryland Avenue
P.O. Box 1000
Niagara Falls, N.Y.
U.S.A. 14302-1000

CONTENTS

CONTRIBUTORS

JANET ANTONIONI is a graduate and board member of KeyNorth Office Services and Training in Sudbury, Ontario.

BELLA BROWN is a graduate and office coordinator of KeyNorth Office Services and Training in Sudbury, Ontario.

KENNETH S. COATES is a former professor in the Department of History at the University of Victoria, Victoria, BC, and is now Vice President Academic at the University of Northern British Columbia, Prince George.

GLORIA DAYBUTCH is the former planning coordinator of the Nog-Da-Win-Da-Min Family and Community Services of the Mamaweswen North Shore Tribal Association. She is now coordinator of human services with Mamaweswen.

PHILIP GOULAIS is the former chief of the Nipissing First Nation near Sturgeon Falls, Ontario, and now commissioner with the Indian Commission of Ontario.

TONY HALL is an associate professor of Native American Studies at the University of Lethbridge, Lethbridge, Alberta. He was formerly assistant professor in Native Studies at the University of Sudbury.

PETER HUDSON is an associate professor of social work at the University of Manitoba, Winnipeg.

MARY LARONDE is director of lands and resources for the Teme-Augama Anishnabai at Bear Island in Lake Temagami, Ontario.

ANNE-MARIE MAWHINEY is an associate professor of social work and director of the Institute of Northern Ontario Research and Development (INORD) at Laurentian University, Sudbury, Ontario.

BRAD McKENZIE is an associate professor of social work at the University of Manitoba, Winnipeg.

WILLIAM R. MORRISON was formerly director of the Centre for Northern Studies at Lakehead University, Thunder Bay, Ontario, and is now dean of graduate studies and research at the University of Northern British Columbia, Prince George.

LARRY MORRISSETTE is team leader of the Youth Support Program at Ma Mawi Wi Chi Itata in Winnipeg.

HERBERT NABIGON is an assistant professor in the Native Human Services program of Laurentian University, Sudbury, Ontario.

LEONA NAHWEGAHBOW is chief of the Whitefish River First Nation and is former grand chief of the Robinson-Huron treaty area. She is also president of the Native Women's Council of Ontario.

ROGER SPIELMANN is an assistant professor in the Native Studies department at Laurentian University, Sudbury, Ontario.

ARTHUR SOLOMON is an elder and an author. He holds a Medal of Ontario and three honorary doctorates recognizing the work he has done in challenging the justice system, the educational system, and other sources of oppression. He lives in Alban, Ontario.

SHARON TAYLOR-HENLEY is an assistant professor of social work at the University of Manitoba, Winnipeg.

Words to the Conference
Arthur Solomon, Elder

FRIDAY PRAYER, 24 JANUARY 1992

I give thanks for the power and the beauty and the sacredness of Your Creation. I give thanks for our Earth Mother, for our Grandmother Moon, for our elder brother Sun and the skyworld. I give thanks for the animal life, the bird life, and the fish life. I give thanks for the water, and the fire, and the medicines, and for the air that You give us to breathe. *Meegwetch*, I give thanks to the four sacred medicine grandfathers, to the spirit helpers, to the eagle spirit, and the deer spirit, and the thunder people. I give thanks for people who have come here together, and I pray that we will be given guidance and blessing, that we will come away from this conference much stronger than we are today, that we will understand more of what we need to know. I ask for Your blessing, Your guidance, and I especially pray for Leonard Pelletier, Nelson Mandela, Winnie Mandela, Walter Sisulu and his wife, for our people in the prisons, and our people confused and troubled on the street.

SATURDAY PRAYER, 25 JANUARY 1992

Great Spirit, we give You thanks for this beautiful day. We give You thanks for the power, the beauty and the sacredness of Your Creation. Yesterday we had the opportunity to listen to three beautiful women talking. They have to do this; we need to listen. We need to let them share their pain with us. We thank You for this day that You have given to us. I give thanks to the four sacred medicine grandfathers, to the Earth Mother, our Grandmother Moon, and our elder brother Sun and the skyworld. I give thanks for all this and ask for Your blessing and guidance again today. And remember our brother, Leonard Pelletier, and all our brothers and sisters who have injustices done to them.

Lisa Odjig of the Wikwemikong Native Hoop Dancers.

Introduction

Anne-Marie Mawhiney

T he Institute of Northern Ontario Research and Development
(INORD) at Laurentian University sponsored a conference on 24
and 25 January 1992, called "Rebirth: Political, Economic, and
Social Development in First Nations." This volume, based on that conference, highlights some of the developments that have been occurring in
First Nations throughout Northern Ontario and elsewhere in the last
decade. These developments have happened within a wider socio-political
context where serious concerns have been raised about the deplorable
social and economic conditions in which First Nations throughout Canada
have been existing since contact with Euro-Westerners in the past and up
to the present time. The conditions have been described in a series of
studies, including Hawthorn (1967), Knox (1980), and Penner (1983).
The high standard of living enjoyed by many Euro-Canadians has made it
particularly difficult to accept the Third World conditions in which many
First Nations people have had to live.

Since 1969, when the Liberal government of Canada proposed in the
White Paper to integrate Status Indian peoples into mainstream society,
First Nations peoples have become more vocal in expressing their own
solutions to the conditions in which they have been living, and their traditional ways of thinking and living have become more visible to those from
outside these Nations. Aboriginal leaders denounced the White Paper not
only for what it did not do, but also for what it threatened to do. It failed
to offer any appropriate methods of responding to the real needs of Indian
people; furthermore, in proposing to eradicate special Indian rights, it provided a recipe for cultural extinction. On one level, then, the policy
ignored what status Indians need in order to live as dignified human
beings; on another level, it proposed annihilation of what status Indian
peoples need to preserve the integrity of their traditions and ways of living
and thinking. Recognizing the full implications of integration, Aboriginal
leaders took a firm stand against the proposed measures. Since the early
1970s, shifts away from integration towards aboriginal self-government
and self-determination have become more commonly discussed and debated among First Nations leaders and between them and Euro-Canadians.
Since patriation of the Canadian constitution in 1982, aboriginal and

treaty rights have been recognized, but not yet specifically defined in ways that the government of Canada has found acceptable. More recently, recognition of aboriginal self-government has been included as part of the discussions on constitutional reform, although the ramifications for aboriginal self-government of the negative result of the referendum on the Charlottetown Accord are yet to be determined. It has been suggested by some, however, that the federal government no longer sees aboriginal rights as a priority. For some time, First Nations leaders have already been acting on their views of self-government and have instituted political, economic, and social measures aimed at improving the lives of First Nations peoples. Some of these measures are described in this volume. What are the ramifications of aboriginal self-government, not only for First Nations but also for Euro-Canadians and other immigrants? In what ways is self-government already demonstrated in First Nations in the areas of political, economic, and social development?

FIRST NATIONS AND LAURENTIAN UNIVERSITY
Laurentian University's involvement with First Nations started during the 1970s with the University of Sudbury's establishment of a program in Native Studies, headed by Dr. Ed Newbery. In 1986, after a two-year community-based study in local First Nations, the Regional Working Group of the Robinson-Huron Chiefs' Assembly proposed creation of a four-year program in Native Human Services. In keeping with its philosophy of aboriginal control, a program committee comprised of elders and other representatives of local First Nations communities, as well as faculty from Native Human Services and Native Studies, guides the program.

THIRD INORD CONFERENCE
INORD sponsored conferences on land use in Temagami in 1989, on mines and single-industry towns in Northern Ontario in 1990, and on alternative labour unions in 1993. INORD decided that its third annual conference should address community development in First Nations. The gathering, held 24 and 25 January 1992, analysed existing political, economic, and social development strategies in First Nations, with particular focus on northern and geographically isolated communities. It intended to foster dialogue and debate between Aboriginal leaders and Aboriginal and non-aboriginal academics; this latter group would offer historical, geographical, sociological, social work, and economic perspectives on community development.

First Nations leaders and academics from various parts of Northern Ontario and elsewhere in Canada contributed papers. Even those papers which described activities outside of Ontario were relevant to the context of First Nations in Ontario.

This book contains selected presentations from the conference. The views expressed in the chapters are those of their authors and not necessarily those of either INORD or Laurentian University. *Rebirth* is directed towards Aboriginal and non-aboriginal people who are interested in issues that relate to First Nations and provides a forum for understanding both historical and contemporary perspectives on community development in First Nations. The articles fall into four parts, each containing theoretical perspectives and case studies of First Nations communities that are formulating their own development strategies.

Part One, "Cultural Diversity and Divisions," contains two chapters, each considering the differences in ways of thinking between Aboriginal and non-aboriginal peoples. Kenneth S. Coates and William R. Morrison examine historical relations between the federal government and Aboriginal peoples of the Yukon Territory. The content of this article fits with the experiences of all First Nations, including those in Ontario. The federal government's understanding of appropriate assistance to First Nations throughout Canada was often misguided and did not mesh with the experiences and beliefs of those for whom the assistance was being proposed. In chapter 2, Roger Spielmann highlights cultural differences that affect collaborative research between Aboriginal and non-aboriginal researchers. Both articles show that those who have held some type of power over First Nations — government agents and researchers — have made decisions, interpreted research findings, and instituted policies and practices that have been inconsistent with, and in many cases harmful to, the traditions, experiences, and ways of living of First Nations peoples. The rest of the book responds to this situation by offering alternate ways of addressing the political, the economic, and the social needs of First Nations.

Part Two, on political action, starts with chapter 3 by Peter Hudson and Sharon Taylor-Henley, who argue that social and political developments in First Nations must be interactive: that failure to connect day-to-day practices with their wider socio-political contexts may fragment and dissipate the energies of First Nations political leaders and grass-roots workers. They stress that strength of purpose comes from a consistent and coordinated effort at the two levels — leadership and grass roots. The Anishnabai (Ojibwe) in Manitoba whom they describe have traditions and teachings similar to those from the Robinson-Huron Treaty area around Sudbury. Next, Chief Leona Nahwegahbow recounts her experiences as a *Nishnaabe-kwe* (Ojibwe woman) through her life's journey and her contacts with provincial and federal government agents and leaders. Tony Hall narrates in chapter 5 the blockade by a First Nation of the Canadian National Railways track in the summer of 1990, taking the reader through the community's rationale and goals that led to setting up the blockade and through the actual events and conclusion.

Mary Laronde's discussion of land use planning opens Part Three on economic development. She outlines the process and the positive and negative results of the system of co-management recently set up for use of lands and resources in the Teme-Augama Anishnabai. Two case studies follow. In chapter 7, Chief Philip Goulais gives an account of the new furdressing industry at Nipissing First Nation, owned jointly by de'Medici of Italy and Nipissing First Nation. In its initial years of training and operation, this strategy has already demonstrated far-reaching potential for maintaining an economic base in this community. Gloria Daybutch outlines in chapter 8 the strategies in her own community for ensuring a more secure social and economic base for that First Nation.

The fourth part, on social development, starts with Brad McKenzie and Larry Morrissette's paper on working with Aboriginal youth, which outlines an Anishnabai theoretical conceptualization that can assist in the setting up of culturally appropriate programs for urban Aboriginal youth. The case study for this part, by Bella Brown and Janet Antonioni, describes KeyNorth in Sudbury, a training program in computer skills and office management directed towards Aboriginal women with children. The program trains these women in life skills as well as office skills, sets up work placements, and supports them in their transition from full-time work in the home to paid employment in the work-force. Chapter 11, by Herbert Nabigon, discusses self-government from the viewpoint of an Aboriginal person. The article provides a synthesis for the book and a basis for hope that recognition by the Canadian government of First Nations self-government will provide a further means for First Nations to improve social and economic conditions for themselves and future generations. The book concludes with Arthur Solomon's powerful closing words to the conference.

The chapters that are included in this volume remind us that changes are occurring and have been occurring in First Nations over the last number of years. The visible debate between Aboriginal leaders and the federal government about aboriginal rights and self-government have been quietly partnered with the planning and development of new programs, policies, and practices in First Nations. These planning activities, while not usually making headlines, have represented important gains in First Nations. The stories that are contained in this volume reinforce the fact that First

Nations are able to establish their own strategies and solutions to their living conditions without outside intervention. That this kind of self-determination is key in the healing of First Nations is shown by the historical chapters, which highlight the problems that have occurred when strategies and solutions have been imposed by outside federal and provincial governments. These historical accounts contrast with the gains described in the case studies shared with us by our Aboriginal authors. It is these case studies — the stories of successful developments in local First Nations — that make this volume unique.

ACKNOWLEDGMENTS
In editing these manuscripts, I have attempted to change as little as possible, aiming only to impose a reasonable consistency of style and usage on the various articles. For documentation of sources, I have asked authors to use the notational system most appropriate to their discipline.

I am indebted to the Social Sciences and Humanities Research Council and to the Ontario Heritage Foundation for financial assistance towards publication of this volume. I offer particular thanks for their advice and editorial assistance to Paul Bator of the Ontario Heritage Foundation, John Parry, editor, and Kirk Howard of Dundurn Press. I must also acknowledge the contributions made by Jane Pitblado, Christine Migwans, Monique Godin-Beers, and Ann Solomon-Straub to organization of the October 1990 conference, and by Jane Pitblado, Ashley Thomson, Lena White, and Freda Recollet in preparation of this manuscript. Finally, I wish to thank Laurentian University and the Institute of Northern Ontario Research and Development for providing the resources and encouragement to complete this work.

REFERENCES
Hawthorn, H.B. *A Survey of the Contemporary Indians of Canada.* Ottawa: Indian Affairs Branch, 1967.

Knox, R.H. *Indian Conditions: A Survey.* Ottawa: Department of Indian Affairs and Northern Development, 1980.

Penner, Keith. *Report of the Special Committee on Indian Self-Government.* Ottawa: Department of Supply and Services, 1983.

PART ONE
Cultural Diversity and Division

Roger Spielmann

Hunting expedition at Pikogan, Quebec.

Chapter 1

In Whose Best Interest?
The Federal Government
and the Native People of Yukon,
1946-1991

Kenneth S. Coates and William R. Morrison

As the old cliché has it, and as the history of the relations between government and the First Nations peoples of Canada in this century has all too often shown, the road to hell can be paved with the best of intentions. The intentions of government as expressed in policy directed towards Native people have been controversial, widely debated, and severely criticized; some critics have gone so far as to call them genocidal. It is our contention that the policies of the federal government towards the First Nations people of Canada, at least after World War II, were largely benevolent in intent; this, however, does not mean that they necessarily had beneficial results. Yukon offers an example of the results of such well-intentioned policy.

Contemporary aboriginal protest and agitation are based on strong and deeply held convictions about oppression suffered at the hands of federal officials, government agents, and other figures of authority who have sought to alter the aboriginal way of life. The litany of grievances recited by the Aboriginal peoples is long and distressing — mistreatment of children in residential schools, prolonged refusal to negotiate land settlements in the north, bureaucratization of aboriginal life, growth of racial ghettos across the country, and so on. In the past twenty years, well-organized aboriginal groups with articulate leaders have done a great deal to show Canadians the costs and consequences of past policies, although they have had less success in convincing policy-makers to change their general approach to aboriginal issues. What are the roots of this confrontation over policy, and of the fundamental and pervasive bureaucratization of indigenous life in Canada? An examination of the situation in the Yukon Territory provides an excellent case study of a process of considerable importance across the country.

It is important first to understand the international context in which the present approach to indigenous affairs emerged. While there is an understandable tendency by First Nations people and their supporters in this country to see administration of aboriginal affairs as a reflection of, and a blight on, the national character — as some flaw unique to the Canadian character and political process — it must be recognized that the process is international in origins and impact. Recognizing this fact does not excuse the Canadian situation, but it does help explain the official enthusiasm for a pattern of benevolent intervention and assimilation by the government of Canada and the swift reorganization of indigenous life among the Aboriginal peoples of Canada since early contact.

Scholars studying a variety of colonial situations, not only in Canada but also in Australia and New Zealand, have noted a qualitative shift in the actions of the "internal colonizers" — those who have the power to determine the fate of their indigenous national groups. Whereas colonial systems prior to World War II involved physical subjugation of Aboriginal people, often by brute force, a new form of colonialism has emerged in the past forty years (though the old methods are still all too often practised). The new system is decidedly liberal and assimilationist, predicated on the assumption that the best thing for indigenous people is to move them as rapidly as possible towards full citizenship and incorporation into the wider nation-state. Sparked by seeming generosity, and apparently free of the old racism, this contemporary colonialism nonetheless has extracted a heavy price from indigenous people, who have found themselves materially better off, yet powerless to control the massive cultural, social, and environmental assaults on their traditional way of life.

Robert Paine, in *The White Arctic* (1977), described this new policy as "welfare colonialism." While different in some respects from previous practice, welfare colonialism is in many ways just a modern version of it — a kinder, gentler colonialism. Whereas the old form was destructive, exploitative, and dismissive of Native people and their culture, the new approach was solicitous and benevolent, at least on the surface. As Paine wrote,

> Any decision taken by the colonizers has a basic flaw: a decision made for the material benefit of the colonized at the same time can be construed as disadvantaging them; a "generous" or "sensible" decision can be at the same time morally "wrong." This is so because it is the colonizers who make the decisions that control the future of the colonized; because the decisions are made (ambiguously) on behalf of the colonized, and yet in the name of the colonizers' culture (and to her political, administrative, and economic priorities).[1]

Welfare colonialism, as defined and examined by Paine and other scholars,[2] presents one of the most interesting paradoxes in the twentieth-century world: the conflict between the affluence of more or less liberal-democratic regimes in Canada, Australia, New Zealand, and the United States and the reality of the impoverished lives of so many of their indigenous people. Faced with the contradiction between the political rhetoric of egalitarianism and equality, and the condition of Aboriginal people, these liberal governments have launched sweeping programs designed to improve the aboriginal standard of living, particularly by spending large sums of money. In so doing, they have assuaged their collective guilt and have distanced themselves both from their predecessors, whose main policy as regards money was to spend as little of it on Aboriginal people as possible, and from previous efforts to destroy indigenous cultures.

The idea that money is a panacea for the problems of Aboriginal people, a universal medicine that will cure all past ills, is part of the philosophy of welfare colonialism. The other part is assimilationism — the idea that the best thing for indigenous people is to join the mainstream culture as quickly as possible. However much the non-indigenous majority has claimed in the past forty years to have charted a radically new course, it is clear that most of its initiatives came dressed in the ideology and values of the dominant society. The many new programs, well-publicized and often very expensive, nonetheless maintained the earlier pattern of trying to bring indigenous people into the national mainstream. If there were any contradiction between the new liberal agenda — expressed in this country by a blizzard of programs for housing, education, economic development, health, and social assistance — and what the Aboriginal people themselves wanted, it was not apparent to policy-makers and administrators. If there were shortcomings in the plans, they were attributed to the failings of the client group — Aboriginal people were ungrateful, needed to be shown the right way to think, and so forth — and not to the structure and ideological limitations of welfare colonialism.

In the post-war period, the decline and death of classic colonialism around the world convinced the Canadian government to change its approach to indigenous affairs. The new agenda did not arise out of a sudden discovery of the cultural richness of aboriginal societies or from a determination to assist in perpetuation of traditional activities and customs. Instead, governments came to see the poverty of indigenous peoples as a national shame and therefore sought to integrate them into the national mainstream as quickly as possible. This process continued until the Trudeau government tabled the notorious White Paper on native affairs in 1969;[3] the resulting aboriginal backlash made it clear that indigenous people had had enough of assimilation and were determined to resist further attempts to put it into practice, however benevolently.

TWO DISTINCT SOCIETIES

The Yukon Territory, because its population is small, and because until recently there was only one level of government — the federal — dealing with Aboriginal people, offers a useful case study of welfare colonialism. Unlike the Northwest Territories, with a sizeable aboriginal majority (79 per cent in 1941 and 58 per cent in 1961), Yukon has had a non-aboriginal majority for nearly a century and has consisted of two distinct societies — a non-indigenous social order, based on resource extraction, town settlement, and government, and an aboriginal society, oriented traditionally around subsistence harvesting. In 1931, Yukon's population was about 4,200, of whom 30 per cent were Aboriginal people; by 1986 the figure was 23,400, but only 3,300 were Aboriginal people (less than 15 per cent of the total).

Because Yukon was home to two quite different societies, the federal government, which controlled most aspects of life there, found itself after 1945 trying to reconcile two separate agendas. The majority population sought a greater measure of self-government, and more assistance to develop the resource-based economy. The battles here were over constitutional change, subsidies for planned development, urban planning and standards, and the structure and powers of the Yukon government. The second agenda, arising from the government's national commitment to the goals of welfare colonialism, sought to integrate Yukon's Aboriginal people into the Canadian mainstream. Here the priority was on encouraging settlement, building houses, and providing education and a safety net of welfare subsidies. The federal government also had to deal with the response from indigenous communities, as expressed through the social problems experienced by a people in crisis, and through the emergence of aboriginal political activism and the land claims movement. The two strands of modern colonialism became intertwined, as the government discovered the impracticality of welfare colonialism and the fundamental contradiction between the priorities of the majority population and those of the indigenous minority.

Aboriginal people in Canada's north, particularly in Yukon, represented a particular challenge to the federal government's new approach. As late as 1940, the majority of northern Aboriginal people remained on the land, using returns from trapping to purchase what manufactured goods they needed and living off the proceeds of hunting and fishing. Few indigenous people worked year-round for wages, although many did find seasonal and casual employment, cutting wood for steamboats on the Yukon River, guiding, and so forth. In Yukon, as elsewhere in the north, Aboriginal people were not well integrated into mainstream society. They lived seasonally in residential reserves on the margins of the towns, attended segregated schools — an Anglican residential school at Carcross or a series of largely ineffectual seasonal day schools — and rarely mingled with non-aboriginal people at social or cultural gatherings. This situation was not of great concern to the Native people themselves, for they had no wish to conform to the values and expectations of the majority, though a few did so and competed quite successfully in the larger economy, particularly as big game guides.[4]

Before World War II, the federal government had administered northern aboriginal affairs with an emphasis on parsimony — its policy was that Aboriginal people were "best left as Indians."[5] Seeing no practical alternative, since Yukon had no industrial or commercial possibilities for Aboriginal people, the government believed that the best course of action was simply to leave them alone to continue as hunters and trappers; this was what the Aboriginal people themselves appeared to want, for they made few demands on the government for support or subsidies.[6] The image of indigenous people asking for handouts of food or money is false, at least for pre-war Yukon; such requests were few and came mostly from the ill or the very old. Although the official policy came from a desire to save money rather than from a wish to preserve aboriginal culture, it left Aboriginal people with the freedom to live as they wished.

WELFARE AND ASSIMILATION, 1946-1968
The situation changed profoundly after 1945. The transformation can be traced to two processes: introduction of the universal welfare state and collapse of the northern fur trade in the late 1940s. The federal government decided to provide financial support to those who needed it just as the traditional form of activity went into rapid decline, thus producing more "poor" Aboriginal people than ever before.[7] The first, and in some ways the most significant, welfare program was the Mother's Allowance, or baby bonus, launched at the end of the war. Although all Canadian mothers received it, the government made a special arrangement for northern Aboriginal people. While everyone else, including Aboriginal people south of the 60th parallel, received the baby bonus by cheque, Aboriginal people of the Yukon Territory and the Northwest Territories were paid in kind. The government believed that they would squander the money if they were paid by cheque or in cash. Although the payments were small — only $5 per month per child — many families visited only once every

few months the trading posts where distribution was made; thus a large family might get $120 per quarter, not an inconsiderable sum at that time. Moreover, the goods given in lieu of cash came from a list approved by the federal Department of Indian Affairs — for example, tobacco was not listed; evaporated milk was on the list, but not condensed milk (because it was sweetened); and oatmeal was approved but not sugary cereals. The bureaucracy, no doubt sincerely believing that it was acting in their best interest, denied to the Aboriginal people of northern Canada the freedom to choose that was the right of every other Canadian.

The baby bonus set a pattern that persisted in Yukon. The federal government provided a range of programs that most people would describe as beneficial — medical care, testing and treatment for tuberculosis, education, housing projects, and the like — on the assumption that it knew what was best for Aboriginal people. There was not even the pretence of consultation, particularly in the 1950s; instead, programs were announced in Ottawa and implemented in the field.

The absurdities that could result from this paternalism, especially when there was more than one level of government involved, are shown by a well-known case in which a Yukon Indian agent named Bill Grant was charged with misappropriation of government funds. Part but not all of the money, it seemed, had been used for unauthorized expenditures in connection with housing for Aboriginal people:

> The dilemma in Dawson City stemmed from the fact that while the funds in the Indian Affairs housing budget could be used to frame and finish but not to plumb the houses, the City of Dawson would not issue an occupancy permit until the houses were plumbed, a unique problem in the national picture since nowhere else did any local authority have any jurisdiction over houses built for Indians.[8]

Grant became a kind of local folk hero, as much for thumbing his nose at the bureaucracy as for anything else, and when he was convicted, a number of Yukoners, both Aboriginal and non-aboriginal, rallied to his defence and helped pay his fine.

Another example was the federal Department of National Health and Welfare's program to control and eradicate tuberculosis in Yukon's aboriginal population in the late 1950s and 1960s. After an evaluation of the problem, treatment was offered quickly to those who needed it. Part of the program, which was launched with the best interests of the Aboriginal people in mind, as defined by government and medical officials, was to remove serious cases from their families and communities and to send them either to Whitehorse or to the Charles Camsell hospital in Edmonton. Many spent months and years without returning home, and some died there. The procedure was no doubt medically sound, and certainly non-natives with tuberculosis were sent to sanatoria in this era, but it carried serious social and personal costs for those involved. Yet few Canadians at the time questioned either the goal (improved health) or the treatment (segregation). Even now, there is widespread support for such interventionist effort to improve aboriginal health, although significant studies have raised important questions about the efficacy of such initiatives.[9]

This pattern continued in virtually all areas of aboriginal life. Federal officials identified "problems" in Aboriginal life and developed programs to ensure that they were solved quickly and that the people continued their "progress" into the mainstream of Canadian life. The goal was to ensure that they had equality of opportunity with other Canadians; to this end, they were to be provided with the necessary skills, resources, and facilities. The effect was often very different from the planned result: indigenous communities lost much of their independence and children were separated from parents, threatening the continuity of aboriginal cultures and otherwise disrupting ancient societies. A secondary but still important federal goal was "efficiency" — an attempt to ensure that Canadian taxpayers got value for their investment in the Aboriginal people.

At the same time, the interests of the non-aboriginal population were also shifting. Except for the Klondike gold rush, which had swelled Yukon's population to 40,000, half again as much as it is today, the territory had attracted few settlers before World War II, although it had continued to support a mining sector. After the war, prospectors fanned out throughout Yukon, finding new pockets of minerals —and sparking a resource boom throughout the 1950s and 1960s. Development of new mines — particularly Whitehorse Copper, Cassiar Asbestos (across the border in British Columbia), an asbestos mine at Clinton Creek, the large Cyprus Anvil lead-zinc mine at the new town of Faro, and continued operation of the older United Keno Hill property in the Elsa-Keno area — all attracted thousands of immigrants, and more arrived to operate the machinery of the new welfare state.

Given Yukon's economic growth it seemed vital to the federal government that the Aboriginal people be integrated into the mainstream of society — to ensure that they took advantage of the new opportunities, instead of dampening local development potential. Thus, over a period of twenty years from 1950 onwards, the federal government introduced a sweeping array of programs for Yukon's Aboriginal people, aimed at preparing them to participate in the commercial economy, by educating them in the same subjects, and by the same methods, as other Canadians; to settle in permanent villages; and to adopt the legal and social responsibilities and attitudes of the dominant culture. This process involved removal of some long-standing legal disabilities. In 1960, Aboriginal people across Canada were granted the right to drink alcohol legally; before that year they had had to rely on bootleggers for their high-priced supplies. In the same year, they obtained the right to vote in federal elections, and in the next year they were given the right to vote in territorial elections in the north. The expectation was that they would in time, and with the government's help, come to take their full place as citizens of Canada.

Beginning in the early 1950s, the federal government began to encourage the indigenous people to become self-supporting and self-reliant by offering grants to those wishing to establish businesses, usually small seasonal operations such as woodcutting and construction. Employers were encouraged to hire Aboriginal workers, and by the mid-1960s requirements to this effect were written into contracts and agreements, as with the Cyprus-Anvil mining company. The government also relied heavily on make-work projects such as cutting and burning brush along roads to inculcate the habits of the industrial age. Some officials wondered if this were a good idea:

> A very large number of the present generation of Indian people of working force age are not temperamentally equipped for regular industrial employment. They have been raised in a way of life which did not give them the very necessary tolerance for the boredom of regular industrial employment which one must have to succeed as a wage earner in an increasingly technological industry.[10]

Such efforts were not very successful, nor were tentative attempts to set up worker cooperatives for the making of handicrafts. The federal government's agenda did not, it need hardly be mentioned, make any significant allowance for the different cultural or economic aspirations of Aboriginal people. Nor did it take into account a basic flaw in employment programs: there were not enough jobs in any case for the Aboriginal people, and certainly not anywhere near where most of them lived. Old Crow, more than 640 kilometres from the nearest road in the early 1950s, had few commercial possibilities, and the same was true for Tagish and Carcross, both on the road system of southern Yukon. Unless Aboriginal people were prepared to move far away from the place of their birth — a pattern of mobility that had become an integral part of the life of non-native Canadians — a shift into the wage economy had little chance of succeeding.

Some new programs were built on existing ones. The Carcross Residential School, operated since 1911 by the Anglican church, was expanded, modernized, and secularized in the new era. New boarding-schools were built in Lower Post (Roman Catholic) and Whitehorse (Baptist). The schools were far more interventionist than in the past, and reports of abuse that some students suffered at them caused a considerable scandal in the 1980s. The problems that they caused linger to this day.[11] New residential reserves, located for convenience near highways, were added to the small list of plots set aside for use by Aboriginal people. And, continuing a pattern from the past, efforts were made to preserve aborigi-nal hunting, trapping, and fishing rights, to ensure that Aboriginal people would retain access to resources that were such a major part of their food supplies.

Government health programs were expanded aggressively, moving ahead of services offered to other Canadians; the Aboriginal people of Yukon had a form of medicare well before the residents of the south. Public health nurses visited aboriginal communities regularly, doctors were available on call to Aboriginal patients, and special provisions were made for hospitalization of the seriously ill. But once more, the priorities of non-native society took precedence. Aboriginal medicine and spirituality and family considerations rarely counted for much in the health delivery sys-tem. Instead, the interventionist, professional system of health care was imposed on the territory, without any consultation with the client group.

The federal government also launched an extensive program of build-ing houses for Aboriginal people. The houses were small and not properly built for the climate, and there were not enough of them to go around. They had to be built on reserves, adding to the ghettoization that had begun with establishment of residential reserves in the early 20th century. The styles and location were southern-suburban in pattern; small bunga-lows would, it was assumed, suit the Aboriginal people admirably, and since they were free, there should in any case be no cause for complaint. If they were abused or damaged by those who lived in them, this only con-firmed widely held prejudices about aboriginal attitudes towards property.

There was one aspect of aboriginal life that the government left pretty much alone until the 1970s — culture. The federal government's assump-tion, a modern variation of the 19th-century belief that Indians were des-tined for extinction, was that indigenous culture was dying. The goal of government programs, especially those offered in school, was to give indigenous people the skills and values necessary to compete in mainstream society. This did not include aboriginal languages and traditions: the residential schools actively and vigorously suppressed the use of aboriginal languages. The government made few efforts to encourage cultural activity in the communities. There was none of the sort of deliberate effort seen in the 19th century to destroy aboriginal culture, as for instance with prohibition of potlatches and sun dances; but those who drew up the curricula for education of Aboriginal children did not see any value in encouraging them to retain the language and customs of their past. The decline and collapse of several indigenous languages in the post-war era, caused partly by the residential schools and the process of acculturation, attracted little official concern until the 1970s.

The conundrum facing government officials and Yukon's Native people in this period was expressed by Alan Fry, an Indian agent, whose remarks also point out the genuinely humanitarian impulse that underlay policy:

> The fifties and sixties were damned tough times for Indian people. The fur market had gone to hell, the riverboats and the associated life along the rivers to which Indian people had accommodated reasonably well, had given way to the highways and highway settlements, and a whole lot more white people with no understanding of Indian people had come into the country. Overwhelming change was underway. Hopelessly misguided though government policy might have been as to how to go about it, the policy of government quite simply was to help Indian people adjust to it all and learn to live as best they could in new ways. [12]

Fry, who was something of an iconoclast within the federal Department of Indian Affairs, was frequently angry at the incomprehension and intransigence of civil servants in Ottawa and recognized the powerful role that the department had assumed in the lives of its clients:

> The burden lay in the fact that so many services were channeled through one agency. We were the single window for a wide range of services for which non-natives would deal with an equally wide range of different agencies and departments. Because for Natives almost every-

thing came through one agency, that agency became omnipresent in their lives. I don't think government per se was the problem, it was the concentration of every service through one agency of government that grew horrendous.[13]

Bill Grant, writing in 1961, observed:

We must recognize that it is not enough to do something for Indians; we must be prepared to work with them. Unless the Indians themselves come to understand the need for better education, better housing, better sanitation, and, indeed, a better community and want to obtain these things of their own accord because they feel they should have them, rather than because it is something that the non-Indian believes is good for them, very little progress will be achieved. Therefore every effort is made to, wherever possible, see that the Indian people assume responsibility and control of their own affairs.[14]

The Native people were not silent throughout this process; there were protests over allocation of reserves, treatment of their children at school, destruction of land by resource development, and other intrusions of southern culture and economics. But criticism of government policies seldom had much effect, since for many years the Aboriginal people lacked both the political power and the media following (which is part of political power) to draw attention to their complaints. They did find a strong advocate in Erik Nielsen, the Yukon's member of Parliament from 1957 to 1987, who became a defender of aboriginal rights, a supporter of land claims, and an effective intermediary with the federal government. But until the late 1960s, Yukon's Aboriginal people lacked the organizations necessary to present a common front to the government and to non-aboriginal people in the territory.

A UNITED FRONT, 1968-1991

The united front emerged in 1968 with the creation of the Yukon Native Brotherhood (YNB) (later the Council of Yukon Indians), led by Elijah Smith. Its most important early achievement was the launching of land claims, with *Together Today for our Children Tomorrow* (1973), which Pierre Trudeau's government reluctantly accepted as the first comprehensive land claim to be negotiated in Canada. Founding of the YNB and the beginning of the land claims process represented a sharp break with the past. No more would the federal government be able to operate in Yukon as though the Aboriginal people lacked either insight about their problems or a voice to express their opinions about them.

The establishment of the YNB also marked the beginning of a serious challenge to welfare colonialism in the territory. Although the system flourished through the 1970s, it was increasingly under attack. The Department of Indian Affairs continued to expand after 1970. A new land claims bureaucracy carried out negotiations until an agreement in principle was reached in April 1990, and a variety of cultural programs, post-secondary education programs, and a sizeable administrative structure also developed. All this has been expensive. According to Erik Nielsen, expenditures on Yukon's Aboriginal people in 1984-1985 were $47.8 million, or about $14,500 for every person of indigenous ancestry. Not all of this made its way into the hands of the Aboriginal people, of course, either as cash or services, for the costs of lawyers, consultants, program administrators, and other expenses devoured large portions of the total.[15]

In democratic "free market" societies, announcements of programs and expenditures of large sums of money are equated with compassion and determination to assist the downtrodden. Many Canadians would be startled at such a sum and might harbour a thought or two about the ingratitude of people who would be anything but happy for such largesse from government. The expenditure of $47 million on fewer than 4,000 people is, however, really a substitute for compassion and empowerment. In this as in other political matters, the "left" meets the "right," for neither believes that money alone is the answer: the left assails the government for placating the Aboriginal people with money instead of power, and the right assails the government for trying to solve problems by "throwing money at them."

These programs, while rewarding to hundreds of civil servants whose livelihoods are tied to their perpetuation and to politicians who enjoy making announcements about new efforts to assist "disadvantaged" Aboriginal peoples, have not always improved aboriginal lives. While it would be unfair and wrong to blame government programs entirely for the problems now facing Yukon's indigenous communities, and while some programs, notably housing, have been fairly successful, it would be equally wrong to ignore the fact that some of them did carry heavy social costs. Only the most ardent supporter of the residential school system (and they do exist) would deny that these institutions did serious harm to many students. And there is little evidence that the vast sums poured into schemes for economic development have created lasting jobs for many Aboriginal people, although they have created stable employment for non-native administrators. Cultural efforts, coming after much of the damage has been done, tend to be in the form of rescue attempts rather than celebratory or supportive programs — the prolonged death-watch maintained over the last speaker of the Tagish language is a case in point.

Nor have government programs dealt successfully with the serious social and cultural difficulties that have overcome the territory's aboriginal communities. Alcohol use remains endemic, leading to high levels of fetal alcohol syndrome and fetal alcohol effects. Rates of imprisonment for Aboriginal people are far higher than those for non-natives, and communities bear the scars of violence, physical and substance abuse, and suicide, particularly among young people. Most of these problems have emerged during the period of welfare colonialism, and there is not much evidence to suggest that intense government intervention has done much to ameliorate this cultural crisis.

It is the land claims process that represents the "cutting edge" of aboriginal efforts to overcome the difficulties of the post-war era. The recent agreement provides money, land, and, particularly, the administrative power to allow Aboriginal people to control their future to a degree not possible in the recent past. While public attention has focused on money and land, the administrative function is probably of most lasting significance. Bands in Yukon, like those elsewhere in the country, have sought self-government and the right to control aspects of their lives from education to child welfare, from management of natural resources to economic development. One of their principal goals throughout the long years of negotiation was to remove non-natives from the administrative process as much as possible and to ensure that indigenous people gain control of the bureaucratic process that so influences their lives. There is no better indication of the pervasive impact and power of welfare colonialism than the fact that the Yukon's Aboriginal people have included destruction and replacement of this system as a central element in negotiations with Canada and Yukon.

CONCLUSION

Welfare colonialism, in this country and elsewhere, is predicated on the belief that the majority knows what is best for the minority, particularly when the majority possess a modern technical education and the minority does not. The altruism and paternalism of this assumption mask the fact that this system, like any form of colonialism, is designed to subordinate a region and its inhabitants to a national agenda. In Yukon, benevolence towards the Aboriginal people cleared the way for rapid expansion of the resource sector and ensured that they did not stand in the way of post-war "progress." And in this, it was successful.

But welfare colonialism carries many costs. It strips independence from the colonized and puts authority in the hands of decision-makers who have the power to turn on and off the taps from which the money flows and to direct that flow. Who can assess or quantify the psychological or spiritual consequences of having the government take your children far away to school, or remove your sister to a tuberculosis hospital, or decide who in your community gets to own the local store or which families get new houses and which do not? That demand for self-government, which really means power to decide on such questions, has been at the centre of aboriginal protests in Yukon and across Canada since the 1960s indicates of the central importance of the issue to indigenous people.

While Canadians have often praised themselves for their generosity towards Aboriginal peoples in the post-1945 period, Yukon history shows that the process was a two-edged sword. While it is difficult to make a definitive statement, it seems likely that the primary beneficiaries of welfare colonialism were civil servants. Aboriginal people paid a heavy price — loss of control over, and bureaucratization of, their lives to an extent experienced by no other Canadians. Having been placed in such a position, they reacted in two ways: some slipped into a life of self-destructiveness, and others, increasingly successfully, asserted themselves in a struggle for survival and self-determination.

NOTES

1   Robert Paine, ed., *The White Arctic: Anthropological Essays on Tutelage and Ethnicity* (St. John's, Nfld.: Institute of Social and Economic Research, 1977), p. 46.
2   For an Australian example, see Jeremy Beckett, *Torres Strait Islanders: Custom and Colonialism* (Sydney: Cambridge University Press, 1987).
3   See Sally Weaver, *Making Canadian Indian Policy: The Hidden Agenda* (Toronto: University of Toronto Press, 1980).
4   Johnny Johns, an enfranchised Aboriginal person from Carcross, was the most famous Yukon guide before the war.
5   See K.S. Coates, *Best Left as Indians: Native-White Relations in the Yukon Territory, 1840-1973* (Montreal: McGill-Queen's University Press, 1991).
6   Ibid., p. 69.

FATHER'S OCCUPATION AS LISTED AT TIME OF REGISTRATION OF NATIVE BIRTH, 1930-50			
Occupation	1930-35 (%)	1936-41 (%)	1942-50 (%)
Trapper	87	85	75
Labourer	9	8	9
Section hand	—	—	3
Woodcutter	—	3	8
Not given/Dead	4	4	5

7   For the history of the 20th-century fur trade, see A.J. Ray, *The Canadian Fur Trade in the Industrial Age* (Toronto: University of Toronto Press, 1990).

8   Coates, *Best Left as Indians*, p. 213.

9   John O'Neill, "The Politics of Health in the Fourth World: A Northern Canadian Example," in K.S. Coates and W.R. Morrison, eds., *Interpreting Canada's North: Selected Readings* (Toronto: Copp-Clark, 1989), pp. 279-298.

10 Quoted in Coates, *Best Left as Indians*, p. 194.

11 For an account of the Carcross school by a man who taught there, see A. Richard King, *The School at Mopass: A Problem of Identity* (New York: Holt, Rinehart and Winston, 1967).

12 Quoted in Coates, *Best Left as Indians*, p. 210.

13 Quoted in Coates, *Best Left as Indians*, p. 217.

14 Quoted in Coates, *Best Left as Indians*, p. 218.

15 Erik Nielsen, *The House Is Not a Home* (Toronto: Macmillan, 1989), p. 241; here he equates the expenditure of this money with generosity and kindness.

Chapter 2

"You're So Fat!"
Cultural Differences in
Collaborative Research
Roger Spielmann

T his chapter examines some of the effects of cultural differences on
aboriginal-white collaborative research in one northern Ojibwe
community.* Within the context of aboriginal-white relations and
the tension that often exists when members of two cultures enter into collaborative projects, these observations may enable members of both
groups to understand better the underlying cultural assumptions on both
sides.

Most of the data for this paper come from the Pikogan Reserve, one of
nine Algonquin communities in Western Quebec, located about two kilometres from Amos, Quebec. It was established in the early 1950s. Most of
the community originated in the province's Abitibi region, with a few
members coming from the Témiscamingue area. Today the reserve has a
population of approximately 500. The majority of families live in their
reserve homes, making frequent trips to their trapping grounds throughout
the year, but there are still a few who live year-round in the bush. A sub-
stantial minority of Pikogan's people are Cree, creating an extremely complex linguistic community. The Algonquin language is still in vigorous use
at Pikogan, although there is a considerable amount of functional bilin-
gualism (Algonquin-French) and in many cases trilingualism (Algonquin-
French-English). Even though Algonquin is considered linguistically to be
a dialect of Ojibwe, Algonquins generally distinguish their language and
culture from Ojibwe. The major second language spoken throughout
Algonquin territory is French, but English is also used.

The history of aboriginal-white relations in Canada has been dominated by white people seeking to "help" Indian people. As one Aboriginal
woman, Lenore Keeshig-Tobias (1990), wrote in *Saturday Night*:

---

* I presented a more detailed version of the cultural differences referred to here at the North American Native Studies
Conference, Lake Superior State University, Sault Ste. Marie, Michigan, November 1991.

I am automatically on guard whenever white people speak or write about Indians. What do they want this time? I ask. What are they looking for — adventure, danger, material wealth, spiritual power, a cause, a book, or maybe just a story? It matters not if this person is invited; the history of the relations between European Canadians and Natives ... allows no kinder response (p. 67).

In my experience, this same attitude carries over into joint research projects, particularly when non-native people are invited to work in an aboriginal community. It is in the areas of respect for local community priorities and respect for traditional values that people of my culture so often fail, not because we are racists, but simply because we do not take the time to learn about First Nations peoples and their ways of thinking and doing things. We are too often unfamiliar with specific cultural practices and unaware of things such as communication patterns, extended kinship systems, ways of being polite, and the aboriginal concept of time.

PREVIOUS STUDIES
There is no question that Ojibwe culture specifically, and the cultures of First Nations people generally, differ substantially from the French and English cultures of the dominant non-native societies in Canada. Certainly there are considerable differences in customs, beliefs, traditions, ideals and aspirations between Aboriginal people and non-natives (Brant 1990, Darnell 1991, Rhodes 1988, Spielmann 1988). A number of recent studies have suggested some of the main cultural differences that complicate collaborative research. Clare Brant (1990) points out potential areas of misunderstanding based on aboriginal ideas about non-interference, non-competitiveness, emotional restraint, sharing, time, and protocol. Scollon and Scollon (1981) write about aboriginal and white systems of discourse and how differences in these may produce conflict and confusion in interethnic communication; they itemize what non-aboriginal speakers may find confusing about aboriginal ways of interacting, and vice versa. Rich Rhodes (1988) writes about Ojibwe politeness and social structure and suggests that conventional ways of being polite among the Ojibwe may seem rude to most non-natives. Of course, such a proposition works both ways.

Joy Wild, Carole Nakonechny, and Bernard St-Jacques (1978) examine some of the sociolinguistic aspects of aboriginal speech and suggest four major areas that cause confusion and misunderstanding between Native students and non-native teachers in the classroom: "openers" and

"lead-ins," silence, forms of address, and "wait-time." Regna Darnell (1991)
considers relationships among speaking, co-presence, and "in-group" membership in Plains Cree society. She finds that (1) deniable strategies are
preferable to confrontational talk; (2) questions should be phrased indirectly; (3) everyone present should be addressed when serious words are spoken; and (4) formal verbal instruction is necessary only for things that cannot be conveyed in any other form. In my own work with community-spon-
sored Aboriginal researchers, we have analysed several interactional strategies, including: requests and rejections (Spielmann and Chief 1986), appropriate interaction in community-based research (Spielmann 1988), preferred
and dispreferred interactional strategies (Spielmann 1987), and culture-
specific methods of managing conflict (Polson and Spielmann 1990).

More important, many Native people are beginning to emphasize the
importance of paying attention to these cultural differences when non-
natives are invited to participate in projects in aboriginal communities.
Webster and Nabigon (1991) provide some insight into the aboriginal perspective: "The process for communicating informed consent must be guided by principles which reflect a community partnership in creating the
framework for participatory research" (p. 1). Further,

> The rights of the community being investigated must
> actively reflect Native commentary and assessment
> throughout all phases of research. Traditional leadership
> in the consultation process is vital in establishment of rec-
> ognized local expertise and is essential to complete the
> preferred role ... as a 'co-investigator in the design strate-
> gy and structure for research' (p. 2).

Webster and Nabigon talk about the community study conducted at
North Slope Barrow in Alaska in 1979. Its skewed results suggested problems in the research strategies used. On Webster and Nabigon's list are:
failure to obtain informed consent, misunderstanding of the traditional
values of the host culture, lack of Native involvement throughout the
research process, and absence of a collaborative relationship with members of the host culture. Webster and Nabigon suggest (p. 3) that it is
important "that the cultural values and belief systems of the host community be respected," that "informed consent be clearly articulated as a community right prior to the development of the research methodology," and
that the research process include training for members of the host culture
to enable them to learn the skills necessary for independent research.

CROSS-CULTURAL ISSUES IN RESEARCH

Let's face it: there is a lot that we non-natives really do not understand about Aboriginal people in this country that we now call Canada. In my experience working in one aboriginal community, I had many opportunities to observe non-natives arriving to "work together" with community members on one project or another. More often than not, the project would be undermined by underlying tension between the Aboriginal and non-aboriginal researchers. I think that one key reason for this is that non-aboriginal people are not willing to relinquish control of a project. I remember when I worked on a community survey at Pikogan with another non-aboriginal. Since I had been involved with this community for a number of years, its members would invariably complain about the other researcher to me, "the white guy." It was sometimes awkward to hear Aboriginal people talking about how white people always want to be the "bosses" of these projects and how they are so "pushy." Suffice it to say, they were usually right.

I have also had more than a few opportunities to listen to non-natives involved in teaching and research in the aboriginal community expressing frustration about how difficult it is to work with Aboriginal people, saying things such as: "These people are so rude," "They're never on time," and "They're always laughing at me." I usually begin any response by saying something along these lines: "In any cross-cultural situation, it is important to learn how to interact appropriately, because what is considered to be rude behaviour in one's own culture is often conventionally polite in another, and vice versa. So it is crucial to pay attention to appropriate ways of interacting and the values underlying these culture-specific ways of doing things." In this paper, I want to concentrate on one area underlying tension in aboriginal-white collaborative projects — politeness and suitable interaction in an aboriginal context.

In thinking about forms of politeness and appropriate interaction in the community where we lived, we observed that most collaborative projects often got off to a bad start simply because most newly arrived non-aboriginal people are unaware of how to behave in face-to-face interaction in the community. It can be as simple as how people say "good-bye" to each other. Non-aboriginal people, for example, use a certain formula when they are done talking with each other, something such as:

A: Well, I better get going.
B: Yeah, me, too. See you later.
A: Okay, see you.

In Pikogan, however, people take their leave, more often than not, by turning and walking away when they have finished speaking. This would certainly be considered very rude in non-aboriginal society, but it is a polite way of parting in many aboriginal communities. The same holds for telephone conversations. I remember talking with one of the elders on the telephone, and, all of a sudden, he hung up. At first I thought that I must have said something to offend him. As this pattern kept repeating itself, I began to realize that *I* was the one expecting some kind of formulaic leave-taking at the end of the conversation. For many of my Aboriginal friends, however, when the conversation is over they hang up. What need is there to say more? This sort of cultural difference can cause tension.

Traditional values are still very strong in the community where we lived, and the way these values operate in daily life tends to be confusing to many non-aboriginal people. When my wife and I had been away from the community for a couple of months one summer, one of the elders, a woman, came up to my wife when we returned and said with a big smile, "*Oh, kikitci adjibonan!*" which means, "Oh, you're so fat!" In non-aboriginal culture that is not much of a compliment! In fact, many people would rarely, if ever, say something like that to another person, unless they were trying to hurt that person's feelings. But in this instance, it was offered as a compliment. The elder had been concerned that my wife had been look-ing too thin and unhealthy. In the elder's culture, someone who has plenty of meat on their bones is considered healthy and strong. Of course, after my wife received this compliment she immediately went on a diet! But the point is that what is considered rude in one culture may be polite in another, and understanding these values can ease cross-cultural confusion and misunderstanding.

MAINTAINING HARMONY IN SOCIAL RELATIONS

Non-native people are also often unaware that in many First Nations cul-tures personal confrontations are avoided whenever possible. Maintaining harmony in one's relationships is the important thing. Among adults, especially, anyone who tries to control or coerce another to act in a cer-tain way is viewed as doing something intrinsically "bad." My friends often said about non-aboriginal people working in the aboriginal community: "They're so pushy. They're always telling you what to do, and they're always trying to get you to do things their way." We saw this same atti-tude expressed on television during the Oka Crisis in 1990. The mayor of the town of Oka said, "Why don't those Mohawks build an authentic Indian village to attract tourists?" In other words, "Why don't those Indians do things *our* way?"

This aboriginal principle of maintaining harmony is also reflected in cultural ways of making decisions or "taking sides," which have sometimes caused non-natives engaged in joint research to shake their heads in frustration. I remember being at a friend's house one day when his cousin, a band councillor, came by with a petition for a certain issue to be signed. My friend read the petition and then signed it. Then a few days later I happened to be visiting when another relative came around with another petition exactly the opposite of the first one. After talking for a while, my friend signed it, too. He wanted, above all, to maintain the harmony of the relationship at that moment. The fact that he had signed two opposing petitions was insignificant compared to the importance of avoiding tension and maintaining harmony in his kinship relationships.

LINGUISTIC CONCEPTS AND CULTURAL DIFFERENCES
Some of the more glaring examples of cultural differences that lead to tension in aboriginal-white interaction have to do with language. Differences in language imply different ways of thinking and of doing things, and they are often at the heart of tension in collaborative work.

Understanding linguistic differences can open up a window into the aboriginal mind and help one to understand and remedy interactional tension. For example, Ojibwe, unlike current English, has a 'hierarchy of person,' which reflects the basic cultural value of respect. The second-person "you" always takes grammatical priority. You can say "Niwabama," which means, "I see him or her," but the construction for "I see you," "kiwabamin," puts the "you" pronoun at the beginning of the word and places the first-person "I" at the end of the word, exactly the opposite of English. So the second-person "you" always comes first in the language, which reflects a strong cultural preference for considering others, be they individuals, family, or community, as more important than self. This consideration affects research methods. I have observed non-aboriginals insist on using mainstream research methods and then being frustrated because, as one expressed it, "These people won't answer my questions!" The non-aboriginal person has learned how to design and administer surveys and questionnaires, but has received little or no training on how, if, and when to ask questions in the culture. Asking direct questions, especially without adhering to community values of politeness, can be downright rude where we lived.

Non-aboriginal researchers are more often than not unaware of traditional beliefs that motivate behaviour in the community. I remember one summer when an anthropologist came to the community to collect legends and stories from the elders. While it was a collaborative project in a loose sense, it seemed that the person assigned by the band council to work with the researcher was not fully aware of what was going on. In the course of the project, the anthropologist became increasingly frustrated at the small number of legends that people would tell. What she did not clearly understand was that, in Pikogan, elders tell legends only when there is snow on the ground — when certain spirits are sleeping and are not to be disturbed. Certainly the researcher was well trained in elicitation techniques and research methods, but she had never thought of inquiring about traditional values and appropriate times and ways of seeking information. After a few days, she departed, convinced that the people were uncooperative and unwilling to participate in *her* project.

Something that sometimes throws non-natives off is that there is no word for "please" or "sorry" or "apologize" in Ojibwe. This can lead non-natives to make unjust assumptions. I have heard non-aboriginal people working in the aboriginal community say, "These people are really rude!" Such comments highlight different ways of doing things that may lead to misunderstanding and reinforcing of stereotypes.

Another phrase that seemed to bother non-native researchers is "*Adidok*" — "I don't know." Now "I don't know" can mean a lot of different things. Sometimes it is simply a profession of ignorance about what has been asked. At other times it can mean, "I know what you're asking, but I don't want to deal with it right now." Or, it can mean, "It's none of your business." Direct questions are often seen as being very rude in the community where we lived, especially when asked by non-natives in a way that suggests doing things the way a non-native would. People would often answer what non-aboriginal people considered to be legitimate questions with "I don't know."

Many of us in non-aboriginal society pride ourselves on being able to "carry on a conversation" to the point that we are experts at filling the air with words. We can talk and talk and talk, even when there is nothing to talk about. Most of my friends at Pikogan talk only when there is something to say, and, while this is but one small area, it illustrates how different ways of doing things, and the values that underlie them, can cause misunderstanding. Silence itself can be a specific message. I remember being in the bush one time with a couple of the men. We started walking through the bush, and I asked, "*Adiejayak?*" (Where are we going?) Silence. Five minutes later I asked again, "*Adiejayak?*" Silence. Finally, after my third attempt, one of the men turned to me and said, "*Kiga kikendan apitc oditamak*" (You'll know when we get there.) Now, that makes sense! I would find out when we got there.

People have different ways of doing things and of thinking. In non-aboriginal society, we like to introduce ourselves to each other by name, we shake hands, we look each other directly in the eyes, we ask direct questions, we insist on people using the word "please." All of these forms can seem very rude in the village where we lived. "What do you do?" is a common question in my culture. Status is somehow attached to what someone *does* rather than to who someone *is*. The common question I heard asked of a visitor in Pikogan was, *"Abiishendjibayan?"* — "Where are you from?" or "What First Nation do you belong to?"

It is easy for non-aboriginal people engaged in joint research in the aboriginal community to become upset, to throw up their arms and say, "What do these people want anyway?" The result is confusion, misunderstanding, and impatience. So we miss the fascinating adventure of discovering a different way of life and a different way of looking at the world. A whole new world of collaboration can open up if one is willing to take the time to get to know Aboriginal people and their way of life.

CONCLUSION

Misunderstanding of other aspects of Aboriginal culture can undermine collaborative research: attitude towards approval and gratitude, the all-pervasiveness of spirituality and the spirit world, aboriginal epistemology, and the aboriginal perspective on the land and Mother Earth.

The research process should be based, as Webster and Nabigon (1991) suggest, on a community partnership between Aboriginal and non-aboriginal researchers. Community members should be involved at every stage — planning, training, gathering of data, analysis of data, and presentation. Methods of research should ideally come from the community itself so that they are culturally sensitive and relevant to the community. Western-based methods may prove useful in the aboriginal community, provided that they are modified to take into consideration culturally determined concerns.

Further, the research strategy should include the training of community personnel from the very beginning. Thus, collaborative research not only answers relevant questions and elicits relevant knowledge but also becomes a forum for developing local expertise. Community members can thus prepare themselves to meet their own research needs in future.

Finally, the community itself ought to establish ground rules for any collaborative research, including definition of purpose, who controls elicitation of information and collection of data, and questions surrounding analysis and presentation of data. Perhaps the most difficult responsibility falls on people of my culture. We must remember at all times that we are guests in another culture, that we are not the "bosses" in that context, and we must respect community-accepted ways of thinking and of doing things. Under such guidelines, the future of collaborative research looks good. Neglecting such guidelines will ensure continuation of the rocky relationship between whites and Aboriginal people that has characterized their interaction since contact.

REFERENCES

Brant, Clare C. (1990). "Native Ethics and Rules of Behaviour." *Canadian Journal of Psychiatry*, Vol. 35, pp. 534-539.

Darnell, Regna (1991). "Thirty-Nine Postulates of Plains Cree Conversation, 'Power,' and Interaction: A Culture-Specific Model." In William Cowan (ed.), *Papers of the Twenty-Second Algonquian Conference*. Ottawa: Carleton University Press, pp. 89-102.

Keeshig-Tobias, Lenore (1990). "White Lies." *Saturday Night*, October, pp. 67-68.

Polson, Gordon and Roger Spielmann (1990). "'Once There Were Two Brothers ... ': Religious Tension in One Algonquin Community." In William Cowan (ed.), *Papers of the Twentieth Algonquian Conference*. Ottawa: Carleton University Press, pp. 303-312.

Scollon, Ron, and Suzanne Scollon (1981). *Narrative, Literacy and Face in Interethnic Communication*. Norwood, NJ: Ablex.

Rhodes, Richard A. (1988). "Ojibwe Politeness and Social Structure." In William Cowan (ed.), *Papers of the Nineteenth Algonquian Conference*. Ottawa: Carleton University Press, pp. 165-174.

Spielmann, Roger (1988). "What's So Funny? Laughing Together in Algonquin Conversation." In William Cowan (ed.), *Papers of the Nineteenth Algonquian Conference*. Ottawa: Carleton University Press, pp. 201-212.

Spielmann, Roger (1987). "Preference and sequential organization in Algonquin." In William Cowan (ed.), *Papers of the Eighteenth Algonquian Conference*. Ottawa: Carleton University Press, pp. 321-335.

Spielmann, Roger, and Bertha Chief (1986). "Requesting and Rejecting in Algonquin: Notes on a Conversation." In William Cowan (ed.), *Actes du dix-septième congrès des algonquinistes*. Ottawa: Carleton University Press, pp. 313-325.

Webster, Schuyler, and Herb Nabigon (1992). "First Nations Empowerment in Community Based Research." In Paul Anisef and Paul Axelrod (eds.), *Transitions, Schooling and Employment in Canada*. Toronto: Thompson Educational Publishing.

Wild, Joy, Carole Nakonechny and Bernard St.-Jacques (1978). "Sociolinguistic Aspects of Native Indian Speech." *Sociolinguistics*, Vol. 11, pp. 34-36.

PART TWO
Political Action

Long Lake 58 elders on last day of blockade. In the middle,
standing, is Rayno Fisher.

Chapter 3

Linking Social and Political Developments in First Nations Communities

Peter Hudson and Sharon Taylor-Henley

Cassidy and Bish (1989: 103-104) have pointed out that a number of First Nations are attempting to implement self-government in the area of social services. This paper proposes to explore more fully the relationship that is implied between pursuit of self-government and recent developments in aboriginal social services in Canada. It will examine the case of child welfare services, particularly in Manitoba, where tripartite agreements concluded in the 1980s established five First Nations Child and Family Service agencies serving fifty-six bands.

A previous paper identified a number of problems with the resulting delegated authority model (Hudson and Taylor-Henley 1987, Indian and Northern Affairs Canada [INAC] 1987, Cassidy and Bish 1990) of social service delivery. It concluded that movement towards a more autonomous model that would recognize full aboriginal control over social services would best address these problems (Taylor-Henley and Hudson 1992).

However, efforts to achieve a fully autonomous model are frustrated by current political/constitutional constraints. Hence the need to examine more closely the relationships between service development and constitutional reform, with a useful a starting point being recent developments in the two areas.

CONSTITUTIONAL NEGOTIATIONS AND SERVICE DEVELOPMENT

Ponting (1986) has suggested that the 1969 White Paper (DIAND 1969) was "the capstone of a policy of assimilation that can be traced to the pre-confederation years." He has noted further that rejection of the document opened up the door for new policy directions in the 1970s and 1980s. He believes that Indian policy has moved through three stages since 1969 — first, "policy retreat" by the federal government; second, "turmoil and floundering"; and third, mutual "quest for self-government and constitutional reform" primarily between 1981 and 1985. Ponting predicted a fourth period of "fiscal restraint and a more piecemeal approach" to self-government which focuses on individual bands. The recommendations of the Nielson Task Force Report and the passage of the Sechelt Band Act have affirmed this prediction. Our interest in this paper is with the last three of these phases.

CONSTITUTIONAL TURMOIL

In 1980, Pierre Trudeau was re-elected prime minister, and the "federalists" were victors in the Quebec referendum held in May. The renewed Liberal government immediately set out to respond to the forces demanding change that came not only from Quebec but from all parts of Canada. In September 1980, a first ministers' meeting on the constitution was unable to achieve agreement. Trudeau had anticipated this and came forward in October with a federal proposal for constitutional reform. Three sections addressed concerns of Aboriginal people — non-derogation of aboriginal rights with respect to the proposed Charter; entrenchment of aboriginal and treaty rights; and a special further meeting of first ministers and Aboriginal leaders on constitutional matters (Hawkes 1989).

Most provinces opposed the federal government's unilateral approach and launched a court battle and a lobbying of their cause in the United Kingdom. The National Indian Brotherhood had already begun to lobby Britain with respect to its special relationship to the crown, which it thought was endangered by the federal proposals (Hawkes 1985: 5, Robinson and Bird Quinney 1985: 39-51). The decision of the Supreme Court of Canada forced a first ministers' conference (FMC) on the constitution in November 1981; Canadian women and Aboriginal people felt that their rights were not adequately protected in the resulting package, which omitted the protection of aboriginal rights presented in the earlier proposals (Romanow, White, and Lesson 1984).

Lobbying by these two groups in the final weeks of 1981 resulted in inclusion of sections in the Constitution Act of 1982, that more fully recognize rights for women (section 28, gender equality) and for Aboriginal people (sections 25, non-derogation of aboriginal/treaty rights; 35, recognition and affirmation of existing aboriginal rights and definition of Aboriginal people; and 37, a first ministers' conference to identify rights to be included in the constitution and the participation of Aboriginal people in this conference).

In December 1982, the House of Commons appointed a Special Committee on Indian Self-Government (the Penner Committee). This committee reported in October 1983 (Canada, House of Commons, 1983) on several possibilities for self-government and, as a result of its meetings with local people in Indian communities, also identified three critical issues for Canada's Indian people. One of these was child welfare.

MUTUAL QUEST

Constitutional inclusion and appointment of the Penner Committee signalled the beginning of a mutual search for accommodation of self-government at the political level that coincided with developments in social services.

The Manitoba Indian Child Welfare Sub-Committee — a tripartite working group consisting of representatives from the federal government, the provincial government, and First Nations — had been meeting since 1977 to explore difficulties in the child welfare system and to propose improvements to service delivery to Indian bands. In 1980, the committee's final report proposed an alternative approach (Manitoba 1980). Following release of the report, the Four Nations Confederacy (formerly the Manitoba Indian Brotherhood) consulted with bands concerning the recommendations. This process resulted in a resolution to enter into an agreement with Canada and Manitoba, whereby Indian bands and/or tribal councils would administer child welfare, pursuant to provincial legislation and financial support from the federal government. Rejection of this proposal by twenty-five northern bands helped split the confederacy into two groups — the First Nations Confederacy, representing the southern nations, and the Manitoba Keewatinowi Okimakinak, representing the twenty-five bands in the north. Thus the Canada-Manitoba-Indian Child Welfare Agreement, signed 22 February 1982, included only the southern nations and resulted in formation of three tribal council-based child welfare agencies.

The northern chiefs were hesitant to sign any agreement based on transfer of control, as it was then phrased, for child welfare from the province to the bands. It was their position that they already had the inherent right to control delivery of Indian child welfare services and that only some existing cases, which the province had reluctantly taken on in the past when life and death circumstances had so required, were being transferred (Hudson and Taylor-Henley 1987a, 1987b). Also, INAC had sent around a circular stating that agreements respecting child welfare would assume that provincial legislation would govern child and family services (INAC 1982).

Despite these concerns, their desperate need for resources to help their people, who were receiving only life and death services from the province, forced the northern chiefs, in February 1983, to agree reluctantly to the Canada-Manitoba-Northern Indian Child Welfare Agreement. They would unwillingly acknowledge provincial law, as it was the only available legal framework. They felt that other options might open in the near future and that they could then make new arrangements. Recognition of this possibility was built right into their agreement and was one of the few factors distinguishing it from the agreement of the previous year. At the height of the Penner Committee's investigations, and with preparations in full swing for the FMC of April 1983, the chiefs had good reason to be hopeful that something further might be achieved. Clearly the chiefs connected political changes and gains with their efforts on services. Proposals made by Manitoba and Canada (INAC) at the service level did not reflect a similar perspective.

Thus the late 1970s and early 1980s saw several constitutional gains made by Aboriginal people in general and by First Nations specifically. These were paralleled by tangible gains in control over service delivery. Moreover, both sets of gains contained within them the promise of further progress. We turn now to the ensuing period and see that the promise has yet to be fulfilled on either front.

RESTRAINT AND A PIECEMEAL APPROACH

After the 1983 FMC, Section 35 of the Constitution Act, 1982, was amended to include future land claims agreements in the definition of treaty rights, to guarantee equal rights to male and female persons with respect to aboriginal and treaty rights, and to specify aboriginal participation in any conference making amendments to the constitution affecting aboriginal and treaty rights. Amendment of section 37 provided for three more FMCs on aboriginal matters, in 1984, 1985, and 1987.

The FMC process continued throughout the life of the first tripartite child welfare agreement in Manitoba. This, coupled with other federal actions (for example, the 1984 proposal for framework legislation to provide for self-government, Bill C-52, which died with the calling of an election later that year), kept the aboriginal leadership involved in the much loftier debate over their rights, as is evidenced by the response of northern Manitoba chiefs to the 1984 proposal. We prepared one of three evaluations of the tripartite agreements for northern Manitoba, and materials that we gathered for the evaluation of the Canada-Manitoba-Northern Indian Child Welfare agreement, including an interview with chiefs on the board of Awasis Agency (Hudson and Taylor-Henley 1987a: 96-97), demonstrate repeatedly that aboriginal aims were much higher than those of the provincial and federal agencies dealing with implementation of the agreements. (See also McKay-Hurd Associates International 1986 and Coopers and Lybrand Consulting Group 1987.) Concern and preoccupation with a system that might rely too heavily on the provincial framework dominated the northern chiefs' thinking, while the province worked hard to fit the newly emerging Indian child welfare agencies into its system.

The federal government was often not a player in some of the important parts of the debate but was moving to develop the same tripartite response to Indian child welfare concerns in other parts of Canada (see INAC 1987). Additionally, INAC realized in 1986 that it must come to terms with the costs of the agreements. A moratorium on new agreements was called pending the report of a task force reviewing expenditures on First Nations child and family services. The task force reported in 1987 (INAC 1987).

Meanwhile, in March 1987, the series of FMCs on Aboriginal people and the constitution ended without agreement. In April, the 1987 Proposed Constitutional Amendment (that is, the Meech Lake Accord) was achieved. Aboriginal critiques began in parliamentary hearings in August 1987 and continued until the accord's demise in June 1990. Almost simultaneous with the end of the conferences in March 1987, the Manitoba child welfare agreements expired. In October 1989, INAC (1989) released a discussion paper resulting from the 1986-1987 cost analysis, and a subsequent draft program directive (INAC April 1991) assumed provincial legislation as the legal basis for Indian child welfare. The proposal supports development of standards of service for Indian child welfare while advocating continuance of delegation of provincial authority and proposing measures for fiscal accountability. These documents also reflect the preoccupation with fiscal restraint projected by Ponting (1986). Manitoba's Indian leaders continued to seek improvements in the Meech Lake Accord and worked tirelessly to make changes and later to defeat the proposed amendment. Personnel in Indian child welfare agencies worked hand in hand with the leadership to achieve recognition of their aspirations for services controlled by First Nations .

In Manitoba, a subsequent tripartite agreement has not as yet been achieved, even though negotiations have continued in an ad hoc manner since 1987. Funding continues, based on annual contribution agreements and the 1985 provincial legislation, which recognizes delegated authority to Indian child welfare agencies.

TWO APPROACHES

Two parallel developments might be termed the "high road" and the "low road" towards self-government. The high road is the drive towards constitutional recognition of the inherent right to self-government which would probably be followed by negotiations around the specifics; the low road is development of locally and regionally controlled social services as full-blown or partial institutions of self-government. It is our contention that the link between these parallel developments has been either perceived inappropriately or not perceived at all by the participants. This section examines this proposition, including some negative effects upon the dual goals of self-government and high-quality service.

There are four key sets of actors involved in the current debate and discussion of delivery of Indian child welfare services — the federal government, the provincial and territorial governments, First Nations, and aboriginal groups such as women's organizations and consumers (primarily women and children). Each frames what is happening from the perspective and agenda of a particular interest.

Senior officials at INAC would appear to be making no connections at all between what is occurring in constitutional negotiations and parallel developments at the level of service delivery. This was evident in the 1982-1983 negotiations for northern Manitoba's tripartite agreement: Indian negotiators had the benefit of participation in the larger constitutional debate, while federal (and provincial) officials had their minds fixed on the only strategy that they could see was immediately available to discharge an unwanted responsibility for child welfare — namely, make the Indian system subject to provincial authority. However, given the ensuing ten years, which included the FMC process and clarification of aboriginal aspiration towards self-government, INAC's continued insistence on the tripartite or double-bilateral route for development of Indian child welfare agencies is less understandable (INAC 1989). This insistence may result from a desire to maintain a relationship with the provinces at a time when the federal trend appears to be to shift more and more responsibility for service to the provinces. It may even be a foreshadowing of the "offloading" of fiscal responsibility characteristic of recent federal policy, thereby resurrecting the spectre of the 1969 White Paper (for example, National Council of Welfare 1991).

INAC took to the negotiating table the issue of controlling expenditure. Costs had mushroomed during the 1980s (INAC 1987), and INAC (April 1991) has now proposed elaborate procedures for expenditure accountability. Moreover, the same policy paper proposes a funding formula that would enable INAC to control and predict costs.

The provincial perspective in Manitoba similarly excludes any consideration of the relationship between discussions concerning aboriginal self-government and those on aboriginal child welfare services. Agreements have been signed and renewed which apply the delegated- authority model to child and family services controlled by First Nations. The province has taken some measures to enable the Indian agencies to carry out their task in some different ways than the non-aboriginal agencies, but it has done that while clearly believing that authority to deliver the services derives ultimately from the province and provincial legislation.

Culturally appropriate service has received some sympathy, but this is distinct from the notion of self-government. Another term used by provincial officials has been "jurisdiction," but this too does not appear to have been understood as a synonym for self-government; rather, it is used to denote the jurisdiction of a particular First Nations child and family service agency over its membership for purposes of administering the child protection mandate. In this regard, the province generally understands the Indian agencies as having jurisdiction over services to on-reserve residents, as opposed to some concept of citizenship regardless of residence.

The province wants simply to carry on as it has always done: fix up the legislation from time to time; pass regulations; develop standards, protocols, and procedures; and monitor the efficiency and effectiveness of the non-profit agencies set up to protect children. In discharging this role, the province seeks to fit the Indian agencies into the existing system — in other words, to treat them in the same way as the province treats any of the other non-profit agencies acting with executive authority granted to them by the province.

One other dynamic complicates the provincial agenda. While the province accepts the authority over social services as defined in the division of powers set out in the constitution, it walks a fine line between upholding its authority and evading political consequences when something goes wrong. A somewhat decentralized system that involves private, non-profit agencies, including aboriginal agencies, in delivery of service enables provincial politicians to blame the delivery agent in such instances. The worst thing that can go wrong is that the children for whom the system is responsible are abused, neglected, or even die. All these things have occurred in the recent past within the First Nations-administered jurisdictions in Manitoba, and the province has been able to stand at a distance from expressions of concern. At such times it has tended to use the investigative powers that it claims, in order to seek a "culprit" within the Indian system (*Winnipeg Free Press*, 6 January 1992). It has been charged, with some justification, that such actions are part of a provincial attempt to discredit the concept of self-government, and specifically to avoid responsibility for implementing the recommendations of the Manitoba Aboriginal Justice Inquiry (Manitoba 1991), which called for greater aboriginal control over the justice system. In only this very narrow sense is the province connecting aboriginal control over child welfare with the larger constitutional issue.

The perspective and plans of most First Nations communities and their larger political organizations at regional, provincial, and national levels contrast dramatically with that of the federal or provincial governments. First Nations believe that Indian authority over social services is inherent, that it has never been yielded, and that the existing arrangement, especially the relationship with the province, is a temporary expedient. The political leadership wants to have full control over the social institutions that provide services to its citizens. Thus aboriginal leaders are connecting the issue of self-government with social services. They present the example of the development of social services — with all the related difficulties — to press the case for self-government with exactly the same sorts of language as they use in the constitutional debate. Moreover, they assert that the inherent right to self-government and control of all services such as education, health, child welfare, and justice is appropriate for any government. The goals and perspectives of the First Nations leadership are clearly, and, given its role, appropriately, political.

There is a fourth set of participants which does not sit at the negotiating table. It consists of the staff of the agencies operating child and family services, the consumers of their services, foster parents who provide care, and a number of individual and organized observers interested in the functioning of the agencies, including aboriginal women's groups and urban aboriginal organizations. Their preoccupations involve high quality service. While the staff, consumers, and foster parents are part of the Indian agencies and may or may not seek change from within the agencies, the urban and women's groups (many also urban) have begun to address concerns through the media and public demonstrations. They claim that their priorities are protection of women and children, and provision of effective services that promote healing within and between people in First Nations communities. These participants see two connections between First Nations child and family services and self-government. They believe that the aboriginal leadership has emphasized political goals at the expense of service goals, and they fear that achievement of self-government might threaten rather than usher in the services and protections that they seek. Some Aboriginal women's groups and urban organizations maintain that the male-dominated aboriginal leadership has sometimes underestimated the extent of family violence in First Nations communities and has even conspired to cover up specific incidents. This concern has also resulted in national and provincial women's and urban organizations requesting specific participation at the constitutional level (*Globe and Mail*, 1 April 1992; *Ottawa Citizen*, 14 April 1992).

SOME NEGATIVE EFFECTS OF DIFFERING APPROACHES
These differing perceptions of the relationships between Indian constitutional aspirations and Indian child welfare facilitate INAC's continued

insistence, with provincial complicity, on tripartite or double-bipartite agreements that subject Indian agencies to provincial authority. This situation thwarts progress towards the goal of Indian-controlled service delivery as an instrument of self-government. In fact, it contradicts it in the most direct way possible and affronts the claim to inherent right. At the level of service delivery, it seriously inhibits the struggle to develop culturally appropriate services, including Indian child welfare standards. The contradiction is compounded by INAC's offer of financial support for development of Indian standards.

Since the proposals for new funding and accountability arrangements that illustrate the federal obsession with fiscal restraint are not yet agreed to or in place, any negative effects cannot be documented. The task assumed by the Indian agencies of healing the wounds created over the centuries is, however, immense. Discovery of more and more unmet needs increases costs. The proposed capping formula, which omits reference to any "override" clause, will clearly limit the agencies' ability to respond to these needs (INAC 1989).

The Indian political leadership shows ambivalence as it seeks to respond to the failure of non-aboriginal governments to place development of Indian social welfare services within the context of self-government. First Nations chiefs tend to become even more enmeshed in administration of programs than is usual under the system of government imposed by the Indian Act. They want to see development of Indian-governed social institutions that reflect Indian governments' political and service goals. They have concerns about rapidly growing bureaucracies that mirror federal and provincial philosophies. Their citizens' needs and demands for services force them into arrangements that are politically, culturally, and structurally unsatisfactory. This problem has led chiefs to insist on sitting on the boards of the agencies and being involved in service decisions. The line between policy, politics, and service is often grey in the best of circumstances; it becomes even more blurred in this instance. As a result, workers in the agencies have to relate to their chief not only as citizen, but also as employer — a difficult situation. In addition, monitoring by the province means that they work for two employers.

Does short-term reform, rather than acting as an incremental step towards long-term transformation, actually inhibit achievement of the longer-term goal? The national chief, Ovide Mercredi, appears to have come to some accommodation on this matter, but he still places constitutional change as the top priority. In a speech of September 1991 to a National Indian Child Welfare Conference, he suggested that assertion of rights in development of appropriate services was possible within the current structure, but he indicated that constitutional change was still his top priority (Assembly of First Nations 1991: 4). Even a statement such as this, which attempts to resolve the dilemma, places service development second. Other political leaders do not even attempt such reconciliation and believe that recognition of self-government must precede further development of services. In the meantime, of course, those responsible for delivery of services (paradoxically including the political leadership) can for the present do so only within the existing set of relationships.

These differing agendas and perceptions, often more implicit than explicit, engender distrust more readily than trust and mutual respect and support. The federal department is concerned about misuse of funds. The provincial government fears that the Aboriginal people are unable to provide an adequate professional service according to its standards. The First Nations political leadership sees all three of the other actors as potentially undermining its loftier goals.

A flurry of events in January 1992 highlighted this aspect of the system. Some children under the care of the system had died. Others had allegedly been left or placed in potentially abusive situations. Some Aboriginal women's groups publicly expressed concern about these situations and accused some unnamed chiefs of complicity. The province threatened an investigation, seeking somebody to blame. The chiefs accused the province of ulterior motives — specifically, disguising its failure to act on the recommendations of the Aboriginal Justice Inquiry and attempting to discredit aspirations for self-government. The province then accused the chiefs of political and self-serving interference with due process. In the midst of this unconstructive process of charge and counter-charge, one of the Aboriginal women's groups publicly expressed its doubts about aboriginal self-government and whether or not women and children would be protected by it (*Winnipeg Free Press*, 4, 5, 6, and 9 January 1992). Meanwhile, the shortcomings in the system, as shown by the cases brought to public attention, were being ignored.

RECONNECTING THE TWO APPROACHES

It appears that participants have little motivation to move beyond delegated authority. INAC is content enough with devolution and has in fact equated this with self-government. The provinces have accepted devolution of services with varying degrees of enthusiasm but have not supported, nor are they about to support, anything beyond the model of delegated authority. The delivery agencies are not concerned primarily with the issue of self-government and in some instances even fear it. First Nations politicians and organizations have their own ambivalence about the place of child and family services in the general struggle to make self-government a reality.

And yet the current situation remains entirely unsatisfactory. The system is stuck at a particular stage in its development, which makes nobody particularly happy. But the different goals and concerns of the parties involved prevent them from negotiating removal of the blockages.

If there is to be a road forward, it lies in the reframing of issues and plans. Much of this reframing would necessitate re-examination of the relationship between political and service goals. Ways must be found to combine and integrate both, so that they are, and are seen to be, mutually reinforcing.

A NEW FEDERAL ROLE

In keeping with the special relationship between First Nations and the federal government, the role of the latter is not minor, nor should it be. No further progress seems possible unless the federal government, or at least its agent, INAC, begins to connect and understand the community-level interrelationships between the constitutional process and service development. INAC's latest policy position on child and family services is written as though the constitutional debate since 1982 never happened (INAC 1991). Despite the very clear positions of First Nations during the constitutional process, INAC maintains that the First Nations agencies must remain subject to the authority of the relevant provincial legislation. The minister for Constitutional Affairs, in contrast, appeared finally to be sympathetic to the concept of self-government and the need to redefine relationships.

INAC's position also appears to be tied to tripartite agreements and structures, thus subverting the intergovernmental dialogue that might assist further development of the services. There is no logic to the association between tripartite talks and acceptance of provincial authority; the two are quite separate. It is entirely conceivable that a tripartite agreement might not recognize provincial authority. The position reinforces the view of some First Nations leaders that service goals can never be achieved in the absence of a broader political settlement. INAC is thus actually subverting the prior attention to service that is its stated aim. This subversion needs to be exposed. Some blame for the federal government's current incoherence lies in the lack of ministerial leadership at INAC. Much policy development has been left by default to senior bureaucrats, who are not connected to the constitutional process.

The federal government must maintain its ongoing responsibility to fund the developing First Nations child and family services. While recent proposals for a revised funding formula are more generous than this present government is inclined to be in other areas of social policy, problems do remain. It would be further helpful if INAC were able to overcome its obsession with efficient accounting systems as opposed to effective service.

INAC could further the exercise of self-government by allocating funds for development of child and family services as an instrument of self-government. For example, the sorts of mechanisms that would uphold a government-to-government relationship between First Nations agencies and provincial governments cannot be developed and sustained without benefit of funds. Moreover, the federal government has seriously neglected its responsibility to ally itself with First Nations organizations in interpreting to the provinces the mixture of service and political goals contained in First Nations child and family services, which are unique to them, and with which consequently the provinces have had little experience.

A NEW ROLE FOR MANITOBA
Reframing for the province of Manitoba obviously must include recognition of the political objectives of First Nations contained in service development. Less obvious is the need for the province to divest itself of some of the hypocrisy that can arise out of the interconnections between service delivery and politics. Despite its own rhetoric, which justifies its relationship with the Indian agencies as service-focused, its recent invocation of its investigative authority to discover why children may have been unnecessarily at risk is an essentially political response to a service issue. The Assembly of Manitoba Chiefs was prompted to respond in kind, and so the unconstructive dance continued.

Instead, both parties should be equally concerned about the welfare of First Nations children. The province, particularly, might recognize that protection of children and support to First Nations families are a difficult task, and then propose ways in which it might help. Assistance could include consultation, training dollars, or an alliance with the agencies to negotiate an improved funding formula with the federal government. The province, in accordance with current tripartite agreements, finds itself responsible for standards of service but with no say in the level of funding. It should retreat from its current response of laying blame, as well as from its belief that somehow political and service goals are incompatible.

FIRST NATIONS
For leaders of the First Nations, reframing the connections between political and service goals involves recognizing that political activity is ulti-

mately justified as a means to the end of improving the quality of life at the community level. Losing sight of the need for basic services such as child and family services in the excitement and frustrations of "high politics" risks making the latter irrelevant to the people. A case in point was the Penner Report (Canada, House of Commons, 1983, 27-35), which elaborated three critical issues for First Nations communities — education, health, and child and family services — but it failed to connect these concerns with the political issue of self-government, even though the latter was the committee's primary charge. As a result, the First Nations organizations that responded to the report declined comment on the three issues, as opposed to connecting them in the way we are suggesting in this paper.

EFFECTIVE SERVICES AND SELF-GOVERNMENT

For all parties, one of the obstacles to self-government appears to be articulation of specifics. Sceptics or obstructionists in the non-aboriginal community demand such specifics, the rock on which the aboriginal-FMC process of 1984-1987 ultimately foundered. Effective community services that rest upon, and are consistent with, First Nations traditions are instruments of self-government. They demonstrate to the communities and the grass roots, as well as to non-aboriginal governments, that there is a capability (quite distinct from, though often confused with, the right) to govern. They also demonstrate and formulate programs that exemplify the inherent right to self-government, and show that its exercise is also distinct from, and in some respects superior to, non-aboriginal ways.

Examples, such as the Healing Circle program in one community in southeast Manitoba (Taylor-Henley 1991), exist all over the country. Most share characteristics that have particular relevance for this paper. All aspects of the Healing Circle program, from its overall purpose to its daily operation, are grounded in values that are believed to be traditional. It emphasizes reconciliation between victim and offender, not solely punishment. Such programs struggle with the imperfect relationship between the ideal and the real — including the realities of scarce resources to support new programs. They do not always enjoy the full support or understanding of the leadership, because they are seen as just programs, having no relationship to the constitutional issue. Finally, non-aboriginal laws or other imperatives often limit local control. In the Healing Circle program, for example, the requirements of either the Child and Family Services Act or the Criminal Code frequently impede implementation of the concepts. The province's failure to facilitate removal of some of these limitations has reinforced the belief of many First Nations governments that the service goals cannot be achieved without total self-government.

Limitations notwithstanding, to the degree that these programs are self-administered, effective, and distinct, they exemplify the interaction of politics and service. Self-government is not just the means to good services and a better life in the community. Effective and culturally appropriate programs and services in the community may be one means to the end of self-government, and therefore deserve strong support from the political leadership, including advocacy for adequate resources to sustain them. In short, achievement of self-government rests not just upon successfully arguing the right but also upon exercising it (Assembly of First Nations 1991: 4-5).

While we argue for a marriage between service and political goals in the sense intended above, they must also be appropriately separated. The exercise of self-government surely implies some appropriate separation among legislative, judicial, and executive powers. Operation of child and family service agencies has been replete with many charges and some verifiable instances of interference by First Nations politicians in planning and disposition of cases, as opposed to overseeing of policy formation. Interference with the intent and effect of protecting the reputation of the family rather than protecting children at risk can seriously damage both types of goals. Such behaviour not only allows non-aboriginal opponents to impede progress toward self-government but also makes our fourth group of key actors nervous about the reality of self-government, even to the point where divisions harmful to the goal of self-government are beginning to surface.

Appropriate reframing and shifts in agendas may lead to collaboration to bridge the gap between delegated authority for service delivery in child and family services and its emergence as an instrument of self-government. New measures should be designed so as to implement an intergovernmental relationship between the provinces and First Nations in this field. Abele and Graham (1990) have argued that First Nations communities cannot ignore the provinces as significant participants in social services. A relationship between equal partners is needed that asserts inherent rights to self-government while recognizing a provincial role that can, depending on how it is played, impede or enhance First Nations' goals (Taylor-Henley and Hudson 1992). Most important, development of, and experimentation with, mechanisms for cooperation in delivery of child and family services, could provide some valuable lessons for intergovernmental relations in general.

These measures might include a joint committee to oversee implementation of any new or renewed agreements. Politicians would negotiate or interpret political matters, such as resource allocation, as well as legislative authority. This last is especially sensitive because of the absence of developed alternatives to provincial legislation. New agreements should state explicitly that provincial legislation is interim and describe a province as facilitating self-government rather than transferring control. A parallel structure at the staff level would consider matters of service delivery.

Agreements might also include a mechanism to provide those trapped in a conspiracy of silence in their communities with access to some body external to the community and the service agency. This body would need investigative and decision-making powers and be independent of the First Nations and non-aboriginal political structures, since it is the inappropriate mixing of politics and service that has given rise to the concern in the first instance. The ad hoc task force established by the Assembly of Manitoba Chiefs to investigate recent deaths of children in the system might be a forerunner of such a system.

CONCLUSION

There is a need to give equal time and attention to the political goals of self-government and the service goals of protecting the well-being of children. The two are mutually reinforcing: each is a means to the end of the other. This paper offers some concrete suggestions as to how this balancing act should be achieved. Any concluding remark must reemphasize the critical role of the federal government in this process and its need to change as a prerequisite to any of the other reforms discussed in this paper. That the senior bureaucrats of a federal department, INAC, should champion provincial rights is unconscionable, particularly given the constitutional charge to protect the interests of First Nations people. We end with a hope, perhaps a theory, that some of the service difficulties that we have observed, especially those involving political interference in case matters, are related to the very fact that self-government still remains very partial. With the advent of the dignity that accompanies the full exercise of rights and responsibilities as self-determining nations, such difficulties, rather than becoming exaggerated, as feared by some, may in fact diminish.

REFERENCES

Abele, Frances and Katherine Graham. 1990. "High Politics Is Not Enough: Policies and Programs for Aboriginal Peoples in Alberta and Ontario." In David Hawke (ed.) *Aboriginal Peoples and Government Responsibility: Exploring Federal and Provincial Roles* (Ottawa: Carleton University Press), pp. 141-171.

Assembly of First Nations. 1991. "Taking Responsibility for the Rights of Our Children" (Ottawa: AFN/NIB).

Canada, House of Commons. 1983. *Report of the Special Committee on Indian Self-Government* (Penner Report) (Ottawa: Queen's Printer).

Cassidy, Frank and Robert L. Bish. 1989. *Indian Government: Its Meaning in Practice* (Lantzville, BC: Oolichan Books; and Halifax, NS: Institute for Research and Public Policy).

Coopers and Lybrand Consulting Group. 1987. *An Assessment of Services Delivered under the Canada-Manitoba-Indian Child Welfare Agreement.*

Department of Indian and Northern Affairs (DIAND). 1969. *Statement of the Government of Canada on Indian Policy* (Ottawa).

Globe and Mail. 1 April 1992. "Native Women Lose Bid for Spot at Talks."

Hawkes, David C. 1985. *Aboriginal Self Government: What Does It Mean?* (Kingston: Queen's University, Institute of Intergovernmental Affairs).

Hawkes, David C. 1989. *Aboriginal Peoples and Constitutional Reform: What Have We Learned?* (Kingston: Queen's University, Institute of Intergovernmental Affairs).

Hudson, Peter and Sharon Taylor-Henley. 1987a. *Agreement and Disagreement: An Evaluation of the Canada-Manitoba Northern Indian Child Welfare Agreement* (Thompson, MB.: Manitoba Keewatinowi Okimakinac).

Hudson, Peter and Sharon Taylor-Henley. 1987b. "A Provincial Role in Indian Social Services." Paper revised following presentation to Third National Conference on Social Welfare Policy, Banff, Alberta.

Indian and Northern Affairs, Canada (INAC). 1982. *Child Welfare Program Circular No. G.4* (Ottawa).

Indian and Northern Affairs, Canada (INAC). 1987. *Child and Family Services Task Force, Final Report* (Ottawa).

Indian and Northern Affairs, Canada (INAC). 1989. "Indian Child and Family Services Management Regime, Discussion Paper" (Ottawa).

Indian and Northern Affairs, Canada (INAC). 1991. "Draft Child Welfare Program Directive" (Ottawa).

Manitoba. 1980. *Report of the Indian Child Welfare Sub-Committee.*

Manitoba. 1991. *Report of the Aboriginal Justice Inquiry of Manitoba* (Winnipeg: Queen's Printer).

McKay-Hurd Associates International. 1986. *Evaluation: Implementation of the Canada-Manitoba-Brotherhood of Indian Nations Child Welfare Agreement.*

National Council of Welfare. 1991. *Funding Health and Higher Education: Danger Looming* (Ottawa).

Ottawa Citizen. 14 April 1992. "Struggle for Sexual Equality Will Redefine Aboriginal Nations."

Ponting, J. Rick. 1986. *Arduous Journey: Canadian Indians and Decolonization* (Toronto: McClelland and Stewart).

Robinson, Eric and Henry Bird Quinney. 1985. *The Infested Blanket: Canada's Constitution, Genocide of Indian Nations* (Winnipeg: Queenston House).

Romanow, Roy, John Whyte and Howard Lesson. 1984. *Canada. . . .Notwithstanding* (Toronto: Carswell/Methuen).

Taylor-Henley, Sharon. 1991. "Community Holistic Circle Healing: An Evaluation of a First Nations Approach to Sexual Abuse." Paper presented to the 7th International Institute on Victimology, Onati, Spain.

Taylor-Henley, Sharon and Peter Hudson. 1992. "Aboriginal Self Government and Social Services: First Nations-Provincial Relationships."*Canadian Public Policy*, Vol. 18, No. 1, pp. 13-26.

Winnipeg Free Press. 4 January 1992. "Suspicious Baby Deaths Probed."

Winnipeg Free Press. 5 January 1992. "Who Killed My Child?"

Winnipeg Free Press. 6 January 1992. "Child Protection the Big Issue. . .Justice Minister Pledges Investigation."

Winnipeg Free Press. 9 January 1992. "Chiefs Blast Child Abuse 'Smear'."

Winnipeg Free Press. 29 March 1992. "Native 'Rebels' Meet in Bid to 'Get Self Government Stalled'."

Winnipeg Free Press. 8 April 1992. "Professor Says Indian Women Have Every Reason to Fear Autonomy."

Chapter 4

Social, Economic, and Political Issues in First Nations

Chief Leona Nahwegahbow

*Ni'iish nii-dbaataan genii gii-bi-kognigoo'aanh gaa-zhiwebak.
Gaawii pane daa'egamgong ngii-zhaasiimi ji-naadyaang waa-
miijyaang ji-jiibaakwe'aad giwi na'a ngookmis miinwaa ngashi.
Pane ngii-maajaami gii-ni-niibing ji-paa-miinkeyaang ji-
zgaknimaang ge bboong waa-zhi-wiisniyaang, niibna giigoon'ig
zgaknigaazwag, giiwsekmigad ge ji-zgaknigaadeg waa-miijing.
   Miinwaa kinoomaadwin niibna gii-temgad epiichi-niibing waa-
zhi-giigoonkeng, waa-bkwebjigaadeg wiigwaas, miinwaa waa-zhi-
miinkeng, noonj go naa gegoo ji-zgaknigaadeg waa-zhi-bmaadzi'aad
gewiinwaa ni-bboong. Gii-mnowendaagwad ge niibing ji-
bzindwindwaa gechipiitizijig kinoomowaa'aad binoojiinyan waa-
zhi-kiikmaa'aad weweni waa-zhi-ni-bmaadzi'aad miinwaa ji-bwaa-
nendmowaad ge ezhi-kinoomaaged wa gechipiitizid.
   Miinwaa mshkiki gii-kinoomaadim. Aapji'sh go gii-
mnwendaagwad gii-bi-kognigoo'aanh genii mkwendmaa gaa-zhi-
gchi-nokii'aad ngitziimag miinwaa ndanwendaagnag, gii-
naadmaadwaad pane gii-maamwizwag giwi.
   Nongo mkwendmaa genii gaa-bi-zhi-kognigo'aanh ngichi-
naadmaagon wi. Gaa gegoo ndizhi-znagendzii mkwenmagwaa
gewiinwaa noozhen'ig wii-ni-ntaawgi'aad. Debnaak go naa
gewiinwaa besho nandnendmowaad yaawaad, jibwaa nendmowaad
wii-nishnaabemwaad.*
   [The first four paragraphs that follow are a translation of
this Ojibwe text, as given at the conference.]

I would like to go a bit into my own background as it relates to community development in First Nations. I grew up in a family of twelve children; six of us survive (I have three sisters and two brothers). I moved
to the community where I currently live — Whitefish River First Nation at
Birch Island — from the Wikwemikong reserve on Manitoulin Island,
where I was brought up. I married into Birch Island and have three children and two grandsons. When I was raising my own children, I attended

Laurentian University part-time, I worked in our local school, and I did a lot of volunteer work in all areas in our community to ensure that my children had the services that they required. They did not experience the same kind of upbringing that I had.

My childhood involved a lot of working outdoors. In the summertime, we did a great deal of travelling from our community by water, from island to island. Each of the islands provided medicinal herbals, berries, and things that our people used for craft-making. During these trips a lot of teaching took place. Evenings were filled with storytelling from our elders, and our medicine people taught us what we could find on each island, so that when we grew up we would know where to look for certain medicines. We also learned where to get moss or birch bark for making crafts and where to find porcupines.

Often we saw our grandparents and our relatives collecting porcupine quills using methods that would not harm the animals. The quills were picked off their backs while they were stunned from falling off trees; afterwards, they were able to leave and go about. Similarly, there was a certain method of taking barks off birch trees. Care was taken to slant the blade away from the inner barks of the trees so that only the top layers came off. Then, after so many years, those barks grew back again, so that there was no permanent damage done. Today when you see birch bark that has been peeled off, it is difficult to imagine how many years our craftspeople have been taking bark from those trees and being able to revisit the same area for the same purposes. Today our young people are not learning those skills — they are busy watching TV and playing Nintendo games.

I remember when I was growing up we had only one meal a day. And we were not hungry, and we were able to do a full day's work. When we went on into school in our primary grades, I guess, it bothered the nuns, who were the instructors, to see children without lunches. About that time, parents started packing lunches for us, and now we cannot do without three meals a day.

A lot of things have changed. Back then, we did not have services available in our communities. We did not have community health representatives, or clinics, or visiting doctors; we all depended on our medicine people to do the healings and to teach us about nutrition. We are looking at how things are structured in our communities today — not only with social services, but also with economic developments that are taking place.

Years ago, many things were happening in our lands over which we had no control. For instance, the highway that goes through the community was put there without consultation with our chief and council. Now we are fighting both governments over those lands that have been taken over by the highway. We are also looking to see what agreements were in place between our council and Bell Canada and Ontario Hydro and whether something was signed that let them put their lines through the community.

Our community, the Whitefish River First Nation, is currently looking at taxation. Our taxation by-law is designed to enforce the jurisdiction that we do have over our lands and to make those utilities pay into our community the funds that we need for positive development. We would like to provide recreation areas for our young people. As well, we want to improve our clinic services and create a place for the elders where they can talk to the young people and bring back those positive directions that they had formerly given to the community.

Because of my position as chief of the Whitefish River First Nation, I have had the honour and opportunity to serve within the Union of Ontario Indians on its board, as well as the Robinson-Huron treaty area, where I was grand chief for three years. During my time as grand chief, it was very difficult to communicate with the governments because of the constitutional process. We did manage to meet with the governor-general, Madame Jeanne Sauvé. Because she saw so many problems facing the First Nations, she responded, "In any other country, if people faced those same problems in those countries and were not listened to, they would be taking up arms." More or less, she was saying, "Why haven't you taken up arms?" And we said it was not in us to be like that, and we would rather be able to talk to the people who are responsible and negotiate and see them face to face. It was her opinion that the prime minister at the time would not see us because it would mean that he would be negotiating before the constitutional talks were opened up to the other premiers of the country, the first ministers. So we were not allowed to speak with the prime minister prior to the constitutional talks.

Today, a lot of things have changed from three years ago. I was at a ceremony in Garden River First Nation last Friday, a week ago, where many leaders of aboriginal organizations were able to sit down and talk with Ontario's minister of natural resources, Bud Wildman, regarding the constitutional process as it relates to Ontario. Our communities, the First Nations, are stressing our inherent rights to self-government, along with the land and resources that come with these inherent rights. We repeatedly asked Mr. Wildman whether he was agreeing to the statements that our leaders were giving. Towards the end of the day, he seemed to be agreeing. "Yeah, this is what I mean, I agree to inherent rights." They kept asking him, "Does that, in your mind, include lands and resources?" So late in the meeting he said "Yes, I know 'inherent rights' does include lands and resources." With that, the aboriginal leadership got up and closed with a pipe ceremony to seal that agreement between the Ontario government, the First Nations leadership, and aboriginal leaders of those different organizations. It is yet to be seen whether there is understanding on both sides on what was meant. So we have yet to read from the newspapers how the provincial government will respond to what took place a week ago.

I have gone briefly over some of my experiences regarding the social and economic conditions that I grew up in and the differences that we see today. Our young people have a lot of opportunities because of institutions such as Laurentian University. They can see our own people working in institutions like this.

I would like to mention as well the necessity to use our languages. We do have our languages, and we are not about to lose them. We want our young people to be able to use those languages. In order for us to survive we need our languages, and developments at the national level are helping ensure that our languages live on. *Meegwetch*.

Chapter 5

Blockade at Long Lake 58
Tony Hall

THE INDIAN SUMMER OF 1990

Rayno Fisher, Lenus "Tubby" Door, and I sauntered along the main line of the Canadian National Railways (CNR). From heavy use, the two steel ribbons usually glisten like the edges of newly sharpened knives. But on this particular Sunday evening, the nineteenth day of August 1990, the tracks were covered with a thin coating of rust. We walked to the outer border of Long Lake Reserve 58. Then we turned back towards our protest camp at the other end of the one-square-mile reserve about 200 miles northeast of Thunder Bay. Only hours earlier, we had removed the obstacles that had blocked east-west traffic on the line for seven days. About 80 miles to the south, the people of Mobert Reserve held firm to their blockade of the main Canadian Pacific Rail (CPR) line.

These actions were but part of an extraordinary Indian summer of activism[1] initiated in June, when Elijah Harper blocked progress of the Meech Lake Accord through the Manitoba legislature. Practically overnight, Elijah became a hero for millions of Canadians opposed to Meech Lake, but particularly for Aboriginal people, who were suddenly given a champion in a system of Canadian government that until then had proven almost impervious to the direct exercise of aboriginal political will.

No doubt, some of the anger aroused by aboriginal sabotage of Meech Lake found expression on 11 July in the armed assault by the Sûreté du Québec on the Mohawk defences against expansion of a golf course in Oka, Quebec. Leading the repulse of the provincial police were members of the Mohawk Warriors Society, intent on gaining the credibility lost earlier that spring in gun battles with their Mohawk opponents at Akwesasne on the Ontario-Quebec-New York border.

The striking television images of Elijah Harper and of the Mohawk Warriors, the former working within the existing political order and the latter representing a radical alternative to it, struck a powerful chord in Indian country. Both alternatives seemed to hold out a ray of hope for many Aboriginal people who were losing any confidence that it was possible to reverse the overwhelming trend in history aimed at their collective dispossession and at gradual dismemberment of their distinct aboriginal societies. Implicit in the defensive tactics of both Elijah Harper and the Mohawk Warriors at Oka was a call to action. Aboriginal people throughout Ontario and across Canada answered.

The Mohawk of Kanewake on the south shore of the St. Lawrence just east of Montreal were the first to support their endangered relatives who were locked in siege with the Sûreté du Québec. The Kanewake Mohawk placed blockades on the Mercier Bridge, infuriating commuters from nearby Chateauguay and Lasalle. Before the summer was over, Canadians were to watch with astonishment television pictures of outraged mobs on the south shore burning Aboriginal people in effigy and stoning escaping vehicles full of Mohawk women, elders, and children. Canadians were to watch in amazement as Canada's army was put under the direction of Quebec's premier, Robert Bourassa, to deal with a mounting crisis resulting from a deep legacy of governmental neglect, inaction, and ineptitude in aboriginal affairs.

Sympathy blockades and vigils sprang up across Canada in the days and weeks following the police attack on the Oka Mohawk. In some instances, these protests involved non-natives who were drawn into aboriginal activism to an extent unprecedented in Canadian history. Many of the sympathy actions soon evolved into demonstrations of local frustration over the unwillingness of authorities to find just resolutions to aboriginal land issues. In British Columbia, for instance, where most aboriginal groups had never entered into treaty negotiations with the crown,[2] the wave of protest blockades was particularly marked. In southern Alberta, a maverick group of Peigan, known as the Lonefighters, demonstrated with particular bravado their resistance to the building of the Oldman Dam. They began digging a river diversion of their own on the Peigan reserve to bypass an irrigation weir and thereby negate the purpose of the dam being pushed to completion farther upstream.

These expressions of resistance to the prevailing trend of aboriginal dispossession were truly spontaneous. There was no one coordinating the actions as part of a large master plan. Rather, the example of Elijah Harper and the Mohawk Warriors inspired relatively small groups of community people to begin taking their own destinies more firmly into their own hands. In some instances, these grassroots protests went beyond a show of resistance directed at federal and provincial authorities. The aboriginal activism that showed such power during the summer of 1990 also involved an internal critique of the structures of aboriginal government, which, although increasingly staffed by Aboriginal people, are nevertheless shaped by funding procedures that tend to impose the priorities of federal and provincial authorities.

LONG LAKE 58 AND THE LAND

The background of Long Lake 58's blockade is illustrative of the kind of hopes and frustrations that were expressed by many Aboriginal individuals and communities during the summer of 1990. Long Lake Reserve 58 is situated about one mile west of the predominantly French-speaking town of Longlac. Both the Indian and French communities lie at the northern end of Long Lake, a narrow body of water that cuts across about 100 miles of low-lying Canadian Shield country north of Lake Superior. The natural flow of Long Lake is northward, towards James Bay. Thus the reserve lies in terrain that is part of the arctic watershed. Nevertheless, the federal and Ontario governments maintained that Long Lake 58 is covered by the terms of the Robinson-Superior Treaty (1850), a land agreement for territory drained by Lake Superior. This obvious incongruity reflects the extent of neglect and inconsistency that has characterized the approach of successive governments towards aboriginal land issues in the area.

The difficulties surrounding the land question are grounded in the reality that many aboriginal groups north of Lake Superior were not represented in the negotiations leading to the Province of Canada's first two treaties (Robinson-Huron and Robinson-Superior) signed at Sault Ste. Marie in 1850. In fact, only three Indian groups participated in the original negotiations for the Robinson-Superior treaty. As a result, they were assigned reserves at Fort William, at Michipicoten, and at Gull Bay on Lake Nipigon — 14,274 acres, 8,957 acres, and 9,825 acres, respectively. In comparison, those native groups who did not take part got much smaller reserves, allocated in an ad hoc manner shortly before 1900. They include Long Lake 58, a community of about 800 members, who share a 537-acre reserve; Pic Heron Bay, 800 acres; Pic Mobert, 33 acres; Pays Plat, 580 acres; Rocky Bay, 33 acres; and Red Rock, 25 acres.[3]

The huge disparity in the size of reserves north of Lake Superior presents clear evidence that a number of First Nations communities in the area have never been in a position to negotiate fair settlements of their aboriginal land title. The legal status of these communities is therefore similar to that of the Teme-Augama Anishnabai in Temagami Ontario[4] or of the Lubicon Cree in northern Alberta.[5] The traditional hunting territories of all these groups lie within land subject to the terms of Indian treaties, yet negotiation of these agreements left out the peoples in question. In each instance, however, the provincial governments involved have treated the land at issue as if they possessed full and unfettered control of it. In the Long Lake 58 area, the government of Ontario has asserted its proprietary claim by parcelling out logging permits to a number of operations, including the multinational Kimberly-Clark Corporation.

The list of grievances that drove the band members of Long Lake 58 onto the railway track had been growing, especially during the last half of this century. In the late 1930s, the Ontario government dammed up the northern end of Long Lake to reverse the flow of water, so that logs could be floated down to pulp and paper operations at Terrace Bay on Lake Superior. After the Second World War, Kimberly-Clark took over this operation. The dam harmed the aquatic ecology of the Long Lake 58 area, compounded over the years by wood bark and PCB contamination from Kimberly-Clark's activities. The cumulative result was that by the 1980s the Aboriginal people were told that it was dangerous to eat the fish from Long Lake.

The rich trapping of earlier years has been drastically undermined by the damage from clear-cut logging. More recently, the Ontario Ministry of Natural Resources (MNR) and Kimberly-Clark have been spraying replanted parts of the region to kill off vegetation deemed unwanted. These poisonous chemicals, the hunters of Long Lake 58 charge, have been showing up in the ill-health of the game animals that they catch. Tales are legion among these hunters of the heavy-handedness of MNR officials whose goal it seems to be to transform native hunting grounds into tree plantations.

During their lifetime, then, the elders of Long Lake 58 have witnessed the end of an era when they could harvest the rich wildlife of their home-land with few restrictions. From the liberty enjoyed during that period of relative abundance, they have been pushed back and back into the narrow confines of their increasingly cramped reserve. Those individuals who have stuck tenaciously to their life on the land have been subjected to an increasingly bewildering array of regulations forced on them by the MNR.

With the example of Elijah Harper and the Mohawk defence of abo-riginal lands to inspire them, the people of Long Lake 58, like Aboriginal people throughout the country, reflected on the significance of their own experiences. They contemplated the kind of future that seemed to lie in store for their children and for their children's children if nothing changed. Out of this soul-searching came a flood of personal testimonials and collective declarations of shared purpose. The statement of grievances put together by the band council of Long Lake 58 is suggestive of the kind of commentary that came from many First Nations communities in the charged atmosphere of those times. The following is an excerpt from that statement:

> In recent decades, far too many of our young people have chosen to take their own lives. Far too many have died

violently and prematurely. Far too many have faced prison sentences and too many have suffered the nightmare of drug and alcohol abuse. While we must assume our share of the responsibility, can there be any doubt that the injustices and abuses we face have contributed to the loss of spirit among some of our people?

When governments continue to patronize us, or to push aside lightly our claims and grievances, we are implicitly being told again and again we don't count for much; that our Aboriginal nationalities are expendable; that we are awkward misfits who would make things easier for ourselves if we would just become brown little white men or white women. Is there any wonder that some of us internalize the signals we are being given at every turn? Is there any wonder that some of us lose a sense of who we are and how we can realize our full human potential in the midst of a province and a country that repeatedly shows itself so unaccepting of Indianness?

Why do we face such ruthlessness from officials who see our willingness to share the land as a signal it is OK to steal everything of value from us? The time has passed when we can any longer be patient with the continued theft of our resources. We must do what has to be done to secure for our future generations the political, economic and cultural tools we need to survive as a distinct Aboriginal society.[6]

As the discussion developed, there was growing agreement that many of the problems faced by Long Lake 58 and the surrounding bands could be traced back to the lack of any clarity concerning underlying issues of land title. "How come we have to do a land claim?" asked Frances Abraham, a 71-year-old mother of 15 who was to become one of the most steadfast bastions of resistance during the train blockade. "Where did the Ministry of Natural Resources get the right to tell us what we can do and what we can't do on our own land? How come we have to do a land claim while the others who came and took our land never have to prove any-thing?"

LAND CLAIMS ELSEWHERE

Frances Abraham's concerns emerged against the background of an enor-mous backlog in the land claims process in Canada.[7] Since 1973, the federal government has been accepting applications from aboriginal groups seeking to enter into land negotiations. Two different processes were established. Comprehensive claims became an instrument of negotiation for Aboriginal people not covered by the terms of any treaty.[8] In effect, therefore, working through of such claims amounts to negotiation of modern-day treaties. The specific-claims process, in contrast, was to provide a means to address grievances of those groups who had already entered into a treaty relationship with the crown.[9] Common problems addressed in specific claims involve charges that sections of reserves have been improperly alienated by the federal Department of Indian Affairs or that the full extent of lands promised by the terms of treaties has never been properly allocated.

Although the federal government did expend some effort to advance Aboriginal peoples' claims in Yukon and Northwest Territories during the 1980s, there was very little movement with respect to the great mass of aboriginal land disputes within provincial boundaries. Provincial governments have been historically unsympathetic to the prospect of sharing ownership and jurisdiction in land with aboriginal groups. Similarly, there has been little political incentive for the federal government to fulfill its constitutional obligation to defend the aboriginal interest in Canadian lands against encroachment of provincial interests. This trend became especially pronounced with the election in 1984 of Prime Minister Brian Mulroney and the federal Conservatives, a political coalition that has tended to favour facilitation of provincial aspirations in the name of national reconciliation.[10]

By the summer of 1990, then, it was becoming clear to many observers that the land claims process in Canada was essentially broken for all but a few First Nations. Long Lake 58 and several neighbouring Indian communities faced the added complication of being non-treaty peoples indigenous to a region claimed by the crown as ceded territory. This assertion goes back to the negotiation of the Robinson-Superior Treaty in 1850 and to the negotiation in 1905 of Treaty 9, covering Ontario lands drained by rivers flowing into James Bay and Hudson Bay.[11]

Since the land claims process was likely to be unsuccessful, the other option available to the people of Long Lake 58 was to take their assertion of unceded aboriginal title to court. In making their case, they could point to the Royal Proclamation of 1763 (sometimes called the "Indian Bill of Rights") and the tradition of treaty-making that flows from this foundational constitutional document. The essence of their argument would be that the crown has historically recognized the basic human right of Aboriginal people not to be unilaterally dispossessed of their ancestral

lands without some fair compensation and provision for their future survival. Moreover, the band could look with some hope to an important
string of judgments from the Supreme Court of Canada written between
1984 and 1990 by Chief Justice Brian Dickson. These findings began to
flesh out the substance of the affirmation of aboriginal and treaty rights
contained in the Constitution Act, 1982.

The people of Long Lake 58 could also, however, look several hundred miles to the east to the experience of the Teme-Augama Anishnabai
(see chapter 6, below). This group asserted that it too was unrepresented
in the treaty negotiations of 1850, when William Benjamin Robinson dealt
also with a number of bands living north of Lake Huron (the Robinson-
Huron Treaty). It was not until 1971 that a reserve was finally allocated to
the Teme-Augama Anishnabai on Bear Island in Lake Temagami. As Gary
Potts, the forceful chief of the band, claimed in 1973, however, the desig-
nation of Bear Island still left unaddressed the deeper issues surrounding
the band's unceded aboriginal title. For the next 18 years Chief Potts's
community was locked in a bitter court case with the Ontario government
over disputed title to Temagami lands.

For their efforts, the Teme-Augama Anishnabai were handed three
very negative court rulings. Mr. Justice Donald Steele of the Ontario
Supreme Court decided in 1984 that it is immaterial whether or not these
Aboriginal people were represented at the treaty negotiations of 1850
because "aboriginal rights can be unilaterally extinguished by the sovereign power." In his view, the fact that land rights in Temagami had been
distributed by the Ontario government to non-natives was sufficient to
obliterate whatever legal interest the Teme-Augama Anishnabai may have
possessed in their ancestral domain.[12]

Judge Steele's harsh finding, which was supported and even extended
by the Ontario Court of Appeals in 1989, poisoned aboriginal affairs in
the province. Successive Conservative and Liberal governments had mar-
shalled all the legal arguments available to oppose the claim of the Teme-
Augama Anishnabai. Officials acting on behalf of the provincial crown
resorted to a host of racially inspired arguments developed originally in
the nineteenth century to justify dispossession of Aboriginal people. In the
final analysis, all these arguments presupposed that Indians are inferior
peoples who are doomed to disappear as distinct societies under the domi-
neering weight of non-Indian "progress." The articulation in the court by
provincial law officers of such abhorrent theories of racial hierarchy could
not help but damage the reputation of the provincial government as an
effective instrument for protection and advancement of human rights.

Judge Steele's lengthy finding helped draw the legal debates surrounding aboriginal and treaty rights more fully into the political forum. Among the more controversial parts of his judgment was one that treaty negotiations were little more than elaborate ceremonies to pacify Aboriginal peoples because "a treaty is not a conveyance of title ... title is already in the Crown." The major rule determining whether or not a treaty was made with a particular Indian society involved the estimation of whether or not that group was contemplating "insurrection." Wrote Judge Steele: "Where there was no concern about an Indian insurrection, the Crown did not enter into treaties."[13]

GRIEVANCES AT LONG LAKE 58

Frances Abraham and the other band members of Long Lake 58 were not contemplating insurrection when they decided to take their grievances to the court of public opinion during the summer of 1990. But according to Judge Steele's logic, the threat of insurrection represented the only effective means to draw crown officials into modern-day treaty negotiations. And it was just such a negotiation that the people of Long Lake 58 sought, one that would confirm their capacity to bargain their way towards the possibility of a decent collective future as a viable and stable aboriginal community.

The list of grievances to be addressed was long. One band member, for instance, told of how he had witnessed trapping lodges full of equipment and supplies — the entire life-support system of whole families — being burned by workers on the order of the MNR. Another told of how his gardens at his hunting camp had been contaminated by chemicals sprayed over vast areas at the behest of the forestry industry. Again and again stories were related of how rich trapping grounds had been made barren and how the surviving animals were poisoned and sick. Parents explained how 58 students had been served very poorly in an alien system of non-Indian schools that received large portions of their funding from the federal Department of Indian Affairs. Young and old alike asked why so many mysterious deaths of band members seemed to go uninvestigated or inadequately explained by the police. The idea emerged repeatedly that the apparatus of the law so often seemed to be enforced against Indians but rarely was the law enforced in their favour. Women told of how hard it was to maintain cohesive families when violent death, disease, alcoholism, incarceration, and poverty are such regular fixtures of day-to-day life.

In the charged atmosphere ignited throughout the First Nations by Harper and the Mohawk Warriors, such ideas and histories poured out in a purging flood of increasingly forceful articulation. For the people of Long Lake 58, a major theme underlying all these thoughts was that they had

never been formally acknowledged by the society of newcomers around
them as the original inhabitants, with prior rights to the land. Without this
recognition, they had never been able to bargain for a secure niche in the
new economic order around them. They had never been able to bargain
for a reasonable degree of access to the levers of political authority, levers
that would enable them to influence meaningfully the pace and form of
change over the extent of their ancestral lands. They had never been able
to bargain for an entrenched role in the management of a host of institutions such as schools, hospitals, and social service agencies, which had
come to exercise such enormous control over their lives.

As the anecdotes and testimonials poured forth, they began to coa-
lesce into a larger picture that told of a major transformation that had happened well within the lifetime of the elders of the community. Social
change had forced the people away from a condition of relative independence, health, and liberty. A culture of welfare, alcohol, and jail had been
put in its place, with untold physical and emotional suffering to many of
those involved.

I tried to add to the discussions by bringing insights from the academic world and from seven years of involvement in the constitutional conferences on aboriginal matters.[14] My research led me to the opinion that the
laws of Canada are being broken every day that natural resources are
stripped from the ancestral lands of Long Lake 58 people without their
consent. The law is being broken as long as the provincial government
enjoys "beneficial interest" in lands that have never been "disencumbered
of the Indian title."[15] Until a proper treaty is made, the land interests of
the members of Long Lake 58 band and of several neighbouring Indian
communities are being, in effect, stolen.

This opinion, of course, is not a new one. A land claim based on these
legal principles had been sporadically talked about and developed for
almost two decades. But the electrified sensibilities among First Nations
during the Indian summer of 1990 created a new environment where there
was a far wider constituency of Aboriginal people prepared to consider the
connection between aspects of their day-to-day lives and the otherwise
esoteric domain of constitutional argument. While most shared the feeling
of somehow having been cheated all their lives, a widening consensus
began to emerge about what lay behind the swindle and about the kinds of
things that had to be done to address the injustice.

A series of band council meetings led to meetings of the whole community in the recreation hall. It was clear that something significant was
happening when the level of attendance rivalled the turnout for bingo.
Bernie Abraham, among the oldest of Frances's 15 offspring, acted as mas-

ter of ceremonies at one of the key gatherings. He is nearly 50 and is one of a surprisingly small segment of his generation to have left the reserve for a lengthy period and survived. But much of his life has been tough, including the years spent in prison. Bernie's gruff playfulness lightened the atmosphere. With his encouragement, many band members, young and old, gathered their courage to get up to the microphone and talk about their hurts and aspirations.

ACTION

In a brainstorming session, a variety of alternatives were listed about how to press the grievances of Long Lake 58 members and of Aboriginal people throughout the country on the attention of bureaucrats, politicians, and the general public. The example of the Teme-Augama Anishnabai, opposed relentlessly by the provincial government in the courts for almost two decades, dampened hope of judicial redress. And the broken-down mechanisms for political negotiation of land issues, especially for groups disputing provincial claims to ownership and unfettered jurisdiction over aboriginal lands, offered no realistic opening to changes for the better. By a process of elimination, the people of Long Lake 58 decided in August of 1990 to plant their concerns for one hour across Highway 11 where it crosses the reserve.

The police were duly informed of the band's intention. At the appointed time, the driver of the community's school bus parked the vehicle across the highway. Several young men placed their drum on the road and began to sing. After about ten minutes, the group was approached by an Ontario Provincial Police officer from Longlac detachment. He told us that we were committing a crime and asked us if we would move off the road. Bernie replied that we knew that many laws had been broken over the years, with the people of Long Lake 58 suffering the negative consequences. And yet no one ever seemed to be held accountable, let alone go to jail, for transgressing the constitutionally entrenched principles of aboriginal and treaty rights. The jails of Canada, however, are filled with Aboriginal people, many of them in prison for petty offences. Where was the equity? Where was the justice? The police officer looked somewhat deflated when no one flinched at the threat of being arrested. In the psychology of the encounter, the weapon of fear was suddenly not his to wield.

When we lifted the blockade shortly afterwards, we watched as the cars and trucks that had been delayed passed by. I was surprised to see how many of the motorists, mostly tourists, pointed thumbs up. A lot of truck drivers also honked their approval. During the summer of 1990, many Canadians up and down this land had clearly become exasperated with politics and elected officials. Perhaps there were many observers out there who, in their heart of hearts, would have liked to have demonstrated their displeasure with government as forthrightly as those Indians who marked the summer of 1990 so unmistakably with their protests. Perhaps a growing number of Canadians were coming to get a small taste of what it feels like to be marginalized, to be denied access to the levers of real political power, and to be lied to again and again. In any case, as we walked back to the recreation hall that day, I mulled over these thoughts, wondering how to present the best case possible to the court of public opinion.

There was a heightened mood of confidence as the group gathered to consider the next step. Early in the meeting, Rayno Fisher stepped to the microphone. Rayno is a commanding figure, still strong in body. He is the father of many children, most of them with families of their own now, and the clean lines on his weathered face speak of a vigorous life spent mostly outdoors. He seems to have only one good eye, with the other protected behind the fleshy configuration of a perpetual squint.

"A lot of the problems we face now go back to the way they put those rail lines through our reserve," he said. "The company never asked us if they could do it. They just pushed the lines through. And from that point on, outsiders just seemed to think they could help themselves to what they wanted. The highway, they never asked us for permission to put it through. The same goes for the hydro line and the telephone line. To get back to the beginning of where the unfairness started, I think we should set up our blockade across the rail lines. We wouldn't be trespassing CNR. CNR has been trespassing us for the last 75 years."

The next day, August 10th, Bernie telephoned the train company to tell it of the community's decision. The blockade was to begin on Monday morning.

My wife, Lena, came up with the slogan. We painted a banner saying: "Let's Get Canada Back on the Right Track." We put the sign along the edge of the tarp covering the eating area of the Onabigon family camp. The Fisher clan and the Abraham clan organized their tents and gear in similar fashion, as the Long Lake 58 protest camp coalesced with every passing day. The CNR had briefly tried running its trains along the more southerly CPR route after we started the blockade. Within a couple of days, however, the chief of Mobert Reserve moved his people onto the CPR track. National rail service was effectively severed. The diversion of some Canadian trains began south of the Great Lakes via Chicago. Canadian trade unionists who were losing work began contemplating their own blockades to force the federal government to deal with the crisis. A few railway workers actually did block the Trans-Canada Highway north of Lake Superior for a few hours.

WHAT COULD BE THE EFFECT?

Was it realistic to imagine that the protest of 1990 could help get the country "back on track"? Was it realistic to hope that the blockades by Aboriginal people could contribute to national reconsideration of the very purpose of maintaining a federation across the northern half of North America? The railways, after all, are one of the few reliable symbols of shared history and identity in a national mythology still awaiting extensive elaboration. These ribbons of steel were once at the very heart of the political and entrepreneurial visions that enabled a transcontinental dominion to emerge from the older assertions of British imperial grandeur.

But the old mythology needed reworking. The railway lines have represented a conquest of geography to enforce an east-west flow of communications across a vast, primal landscape. Brian Mulroney's free trade treaty with the United States, however, rendered old ideals obsolete. The country was in need of new rationales to justify elaboration of a Canadian nationality even as the full authority of official sanction was lent to extensive development of commercial activity along trans-national corridors running from north to south and from south to north.

The stoppage of traffic created a moment of heightened contemplation all up and down the tracks. After a century of quiet accommodation, why had two obscure Indian bands in Northern Ontario suddenly withdrawn their acquiescence to the flow of commerce across their lands? How strong was the frustration that had forced the people onto the tracks? What was the strength of their resolve? How contagious was it? How organized were they? How strongly were the actions in Northern Ontario connected to what was happening in Oka or in British Columbia? What might Aboriginal people do next? Who would join in? Was the protest legitimate, or was the action an insupportable assault on Canada's civil and economic order? You could almost feel the intensity of the questioning pass along the rails like an electric current.

Who was in a stronger position than Aboriginal people to call into being a fresh vision of Canada's future? Who was in a stronger position to bring a knowing eye to conceptions of nation building than those who for 500 years have been harshly pushed aside and treated as though they were primitive obstacles in the way of the arrogant newcomers' bulldozer "progress"? What more evocative symbol of national development could there be than the railway, that hefty engine of communications that opened First Nations land to large-scale penetration of peoples, cultures, and legal traditions imported largely from Europe?

What would be the chemistry of mixing the politics of railways with the politics of Indianness? Might some kind of formula result from the blockade that would help get Canada back on the right track? Or was the imagery of masked Mohawk Warriors so overpowering as to blank out receptiveness to the broader range of ideas coming forth from Aboriginal people during their summer of 1990?

EVENTS OF THE BLOCKADE

Ronnie Towegishig brought in the hind quarter of a moose when we were first setting up the protest camp. Later in the week, someone contributed two large sturgeon to our communal food supply. Once the camp got going, an easy rhythm took over. During that part of the summer, most of the people of Long Lake 58 lived outside anyway. Some of the elders simply stayed in their tents beside the classic old Catholic church on the point jutting out from the north shore of Long Lake. Every day the elders walked the half mile or so between the point and the protest camp at the northern edge of the train yard on the reserve.

Early on, we had come to a good understanding with the Ontario Provincial Police (OPP) — they would allow every opportunity for peaceful resolution of the matter through rational negotiation. A provincial election was under way, and there were sound motives for politicians in the provincial government to see that the whole affair did not explode in their faces.

Largely as a result of Frankie Onabigon's insistence, a meeting took place mid-week between the area's aboriginal leadership and Longlac's town council. We wanted to do everything in our power to avoid the kind of ugly racial confrontations that had been taking place in Oka and Chateauguay. Using a large map of the area, we tried to describe what was involved in the assertion of aboriginal title. We tried to provide reassurance that non-Indians had nothing to fear from just resolution of the land dispute. In fact, it was my contention that everyone in the Longlac area stood to benefit from the economic rejuvenation that would probably develop in the aftermath of a modern-day treaty.

On 13 August, when we entered the CNR train yard on the reserve, Mr. Brad Lee, an executive of the federal crown corporation, was there to meet us. He was accompanied by a CNR police officer. When we convinced Mr. Lee of our resolve to persist with our plans, he announced his intention to advise head office to close the line. The gesture that he made when he declared this decision reminded me of a baseball umpire signalling that the runner was safe at first base.

Later in the afternoon, Mr. Lee met with the band council. He requested a letter outlining specific actions that the CNR might take to the federal government to bring the blockade to an early end. By the following morning, we had a single page that asked the federal minister of transport to bring our grievances to the prime minister's attention. In addition, we asked the company to describe its view of the nature of its title to Long Lake 58 reserve lands. Similarly, we asked CNR to give us its legal opinion concerning the nature of its claim to land under the tracks in those parts of the country where aboriginal title remains unceded.

We marked our delivery of the letter to the CNR by raising a banner. It asked simply, "Who's Trespassing?" In Elder Rayno Fisher's mind, there was no doubt. He kept repeating his reassurance, "We're not trespassing on CNR. They've been trespassing on us for 75 years." Our strategy was to reverse the logic of land claims. For once, the onus would be on groups other than Aboriginal people to prove the legitimacy of *their* land claim. Let the federal crown corporation prove the legitimacy of its claim to a federal Indian reserve.

With the passing hours and days, our web of communications from the band office widened dramatically. A stream of inquiries from the media turned into a flood. Then reporters began to show up in person. By the end of the week, CBC, CTV and the Global television network sent crews out to the camp. We even fielded a telephone call from the *Wall Street Journal*.

We also established contact with the office of Ian Scott, attorney-general of Ontario and minister of native affairs, who had left the campaign trail to deal with the blockades. In telephone discussions with his officials, we soon arrived at a consensus that a major part of the problem lay with the federal government. Although aboriginal land matters are the explicit constitutional responsibility of Ottawa, there was no political will there even to initiate a negotiating process. We agreed with officials in Mr. Scott's office that both Indians and the government of Ontario shared an interest in inducing the federal government to deal constructively with unresolved aboriginal land issues.

By 16 August, we reached a bottleneck in negotiations. Since we were appealing ultimately to the court of public opinion, we had to show a good degree of consistency and moderation in our assertions. We tried to get word out that we would allow VIA passenger trains through the blockade, but not cargo trains. This offer was never acknowledged. We also reasoned that it was unrealistic to expect immediate movement on the larger land issue. As we informed Mr. Lee, all that would be required for us to break the camp would be a letter from the minister of transport, Doug Lewis, that acknowledged that there might be some legal uncertainties concerning the overlapping title of the CNR to Long Lake 58 reserve lands. Such an acknowledgment, we reasoned, would eventually set in motion a chain of events that would necessitate federal involvement in the more general land issue.

It seemed to us that we could force the federal government's hand by focusing on the nature of CNR's claim to Long Lake 58 reserve lands, thereby eliminating the argument of federal-provincial jurisdictional overlap which is the federal government's usual justification for inaction on Indian land issues. CNR is a federal crown corporation; rail transport is a federal responsibility in our constitution. Indians are federal creatures, according to the Victorian logic of the British North America Act 1867, and Indian reserves have long been treated as federal domains. Putting this Indian issue in an exclusively federal frame of reference should have prevented federal officials from claiming that their hands were tied because provinces in Canada have jurisdiction over natural resources.

It did not take long for Doug Lewis to signal his response to our offer. Lena and I were driving over to the protest camp for a community meeting, when suddenly there was a news bulletin over the car radio. "A spokesperson for Transport Minister Doug Lewis announced that the OPP and CNR police have been asked to do whatever is necessary to remove the Native blockade on the CNR line at Longlac, Ontario."

We arrived at the camp and parked the car. A few minutes later, the OPP helicopter hovered overhead. Perhaps the observers above were watching in the expectation that the group would break apart out of fear. What they witnessed instead was a movement of vehicles and people towards the camp. By this point, many people at Long Lake 58 had decided that they wanted to be included if some were to be arrested.

We held the meeting as planned, fully expecting the police to arrive at any minute. The air was languid with humidity, as if it were about to rain. In this dense, tense atmosphere, many of the most moving speeches were made. The train yard was wired with electricity, so we could put the band's public address system to good use. Several young people came forward who had not yet spoken in the community gatherings. Diane Abraham talked with particular resolve about standing proud together in the face of intimidation. So much had been stripped from the people, but here was a chance to regain a measure of dignity in the face of all the abuse. Diane's son, "the professor," also said a few words. Again and again the importance of holding together was stressed. It was natural to feel afraid, said Tubby Door, but it would be wrong now to be ruled by that fear. Tubby's more serious contributions to the deliberations were always lightened by his infectious giggle.

The police did not come in. Somewhere in the chain of command, probably at Ian Scott's office, the federal order was flatly refused. We had passed through the bottleneck without losing ground. We could relax a little.

Mr. Lee's role as go-between with the company and, indirectly, with the federal government came to an end that day. In a small ceremony, we acknowledged the congenial diplomacy that he brought to the affair. As Mr. Lee left the scene, a new player entered. Mitch Phillips presented himself as the district manager of the Department of Indian Affairs and Northern Development's (DIAND's) Thunder Bay office. Essentially he was the modern personification of Long Lake 58's Indian agent.

"Mitch" introduced himself at the microphone. He began by apologizing for the fact that in his years of service he had never actually visited the reserve. After these remarks, the 'Indian agent' had to face a lot of questions from the audience of strangers before him. The harshest commentary came from Bernie Abraham. He took the microphone from Mr. Phillips, a small man, and made his gruff accusations only inches away from the Indian agent's nose. The photographer from the *Toronto Star* caught the encounter in a photograph that was widely distributed over the wire services. An image was captured of the moment when remote officialdom in

Lena ONabigon, Thunder Bay

Confrontation between Bernard Abraham and Mitch Phillips, district manager of DIAND.

Lena ONabigon, Thunder Bay

Negotiations with the OPP took place in the Ojibwe language.

the Indian Affairs Department was finally cornered into a symbolic act of accountability to the people on the receiving end of the federal government's arbitrary rule.

Friday was the day when the television crews descended on the camp. The television journalists seem to move in a pack. By Friday evening they had all left, just as events began to reach a climax.

The atmosphere at the camp on Saturday morning was especially calm. For some reason, all the old people were there. Several of these elders of the Ojibwe I had not seen before. They seemed to share a satisfied air of quiet understanding. There were several comments about how Mrs. Abraham looked healthier than she had looked in years. In her bright, patterned garments of plaid and paisley, she cut a striking figure. A number of her 15 children were among the mainstays of our action during a week that was for many of us one of the most intensely memorable experiences of our lives.

THE INJUNCTION
It was a good moment for the elders to have been there in such numbers. The police officer of the CNR, with whom we had become reasonably friendly, walked into the camp with a thick file under his arm. In the file

were xerox copies of an injunction. The injunction had been granted earlier that morning to the CNR by Mr. Justice Joseph O'Driscoll of the Supreme Court of Ontario. The defendants were listed as Sidney Abraham, Bernard Abraham, Jocelyn Bouchard, Judy Desmoulin, Allan Towegishig, Veronica Waboose, Frank Onabigon, Rick Desmoulin, Ronald Towegishig, Tony Hall and "All Members of the Long Lake 58 Reserve Band and the Council Thereof." The document accused us of "trespassing" upon "property owned by or entrusted to the Plaintiff," including the tracks, the right of way, and the "wye lands situate in and about Long Lake 58 Reserve." The wye lands cover the rail yard between the two major lines on the reserve, one running to Thunder Bay and the other to Winnipeg. Between these lines runs a circular connecting line where trains can turn around. What Judge O'Driscoll demanded was that the camp be entirely removed from the wye lands.

A turning point had arrived. The CNR man made a short announcement of his intention to serve individuals with a copy of the injunction. I moved quickly to the microphone to respond to his remarks. I suggested that only those individuals who felt entirely comfortable communicating in English should accept the injunction. I continued by indicating that those individuals who were more fluent in Ojibwe should not accept the document. Rather they should wait until translation services were provided to explain the court ruling in the Ojibwe tongue. The suggestion, I thought, was a fair one. Throughout their lives, the elders had been subjected to the imposition from afar of a bewildering array of rules and regulations that they were expected to follow. Often these rules were enforced extremely arbitrarily, even heavy-handedly, without sufficient explanation. What was the basis of the authority to which they were always expected to submit? Why was it that their own language, culture, and beliefs were never considered a legitimate factor to be taken into account in the raw exercise of power?

The chief and council, who along with myself had been named individually in the injunction, retired into the school bus parked at the camp. Already the bus had proved useful when groups of individuals at the camp wanted to meet privately. The band's lawyer, Marty Minuke, who had recently arrived from Winnipeg, gave us his view of the injunction's meaning. We asked one another about the ethics of what we should tell the elders. We reasoned that as long as the elders remained uncertain about the meaning of the injunction, it could not be legally enforced on them. It was only logical, we reasoned further, that the explanation of the injunction should be provided in Ojibwe by those with responsibility for enforcing the court order. The decision was formalized with a show of hands.

Although Marty Minuke was dubious, we decided to make a stand on the language issue.

The group also passed a band council resolution asking Mitch Phillips to go to his superiors at the Department of Indian Affairs to seek funding to meet the legal difficulties of the band. That seemed an appropriate role for the Indian agent. After all, since the council was specifically mentioned in the injunction, and since band councils in Canadian law are technically administrative extensions of the Department of Indian Affairs, the injunction was directed as much at the federal government as at us personally.

The court order changed the picture dramatically for the police. Their hand was being forced. Apparently the Longlac town council had agreed to make the Sportsplex, the biggest building in town, available to the OPP. It was possible that the hockey arena would have to be transformed into an incarceration centre. A major police operation was quietly set in motion. There were different estimates going around about the number of officers involved. No doubt there were also a number of contingency plans involving different scenarios about the amount of resistance that the police would meet if they were forced to break up the camp physically. My impression is that about 230 officers were involved, a major contingent in sparsely settled Northern Ontario.

Now the emotional temperature really started to rise quickly. I tried to keep calm by going on one of my solitary walks along the quiet, empty track. After having spent the winter on the bald prairie at Lethbridge, I still found a lot of rejuvenating solace amid the thick forest lands of the Pre-Cambrian Shield.

When I got back to the camp, I witnessed a remarkable spectacle under way. Two Aboriginal OPP officers were sitting at a table engaged in intense discussion. Across the table from them was a council of elders, with Rayno Fisher squarely in the middle. The younger officer, Constable Larry Indian from Kenora, was endeavouring to explain the complex legal phraseology of the injunction in the Ojibwe language. The experience clearly was not easy for him. The elders seemed to be calling him to account for being on the opposite side of the table. Beside Constable Indian sat a distinguished-looking older man with grey hair and green eyes. He later told me that he was Saulteaux from Fort Alexander Reserve in Manitoba. Inspector Rupert did not speak the Ojibwe language.

In the hours ahead, I came to see this officer as an effective interpreter of the band's position to the chain of command controlling the OPP contingent in the Sportsplex. He was in a tough position, and, to my way of thinking, he rose to the challenge. His actions persuaded me that it is possible to work as an effective advocate of aboriginal interests from within the police.

Although I missed most of the specifics of this Ojibwe discussion, I sensed a most serious gravity in what was being said. Obviously, the matters at issue went far beyond the specifics of the injunction. A group of Aboriginal people were really getting near the heart of the dilemma of how to cope with the massive intrusion of white people's power in their midst. Constable Indian wore the uniform of the crown but in this context he became part of a deeper community of shared aboriginal interest with which he was forced to deal. Many onlookers listened intensely. Most of the younger people still understood Ojibwe to some extent, even if they did not often speak the language.

You could almost feel the ideas crackling in the air after the meeting. What should be done? When I spoke with Mrs. Abraham, she was clearly distraught. "Where is the CNR's evidence?" she asked. "How come they don't have to show any evidence? How come we always have to show evidence but they don't?" Of course that query got near the heart of the matter. I took Frances Abraham's hand, and we walked over to Constable Indian, to whom she restated her question. There was not much that he could say.

Marty Minuke went with Bernie Abraham to the Sportsplex on the morning of 19 August. The two understood each other well. At a community gathering later that morning, Marty told us about the meeting with the OPP at the Sportsplex. He began by speaking of the "sea of blue uniforms" in the hockey arena. The police officers with whom he had spoken began by acknowledging the peacefulness of our action and the absolute absence of property damage. In retrospect, I believe that the discipline that we had shown in this regard became one of our strongest bargaining points. If even one of the young people had succumbed to a small act of destruction, the pretext would have been provided to move on all of us, with the justification that police intervention was a protective measure.

Marty proceeded to outline the terms of the ultimatum given us by the police. If we did not move our protest camp within several hours, we would be arrested for violating the injunction. Over the course of the day, we faced a further succession of ultimatums, demanding that we give way to the law within shrinking time frames. We balanced consideration of the ultimatums with our awareness that the OPP were really committed to search for a way out of the impasse without the use of force. There would certainly be unpredictable political consequences if the province's police force were to be photographed taking into custody a whole Indian band, including elders and children, for trespassing on their own reserve. The imagery would hardly enhance public perceptions of the police or of the chain of command above them. The spectacle would have represented an embarrassment especially for Ian Scott, the minister of native affairs, who was also the elected official ultimately in charge of the OPP.

There was an amazing chemistry that took hold of the committed souls at the camp during the hours that followed. The people divided and regrouped into a fascinating variety of entities and interests. At one point, the elders wanted to meet in private along with Bernie in the school bus. At other points, the chief and council met in the bus. Informal family gatherings also developed. Roy Michano, the thoughtful chief of Pic-Heron Bay, seemed to take it as his special responsibility to include the young people in the decision-making and to stimulate discussion of the larger context of the present controversy. Throughout the affair, Chief Michano provided guidance and support in a quiet but effective way. The concept of self-determination began to take on new meaning for me.

Some of the elders, including Frances Abraham, stuck to their hard and fast positions. So too did Frankie and Councillor Judy Desmoulin, an energetic young leader who provided much of the administrative know-how for the band. The possibility of being arrested was in a sense our strongest weapon. There was a strongly held school of thought that we should force the government into bringing down the full weight of its law enforcement agencies upon us. Another community of interest saw wisdom in a less confrontational end to the affair. Those inclined to this approach argued that we had made our point and that it was time to pull back a little, in the expectation that others would find their own ways to continue the pressure. As the issues were clarified through this intense exchange of ideas, there seemed to be a growing possibility of finding middle ground.

In the late afternoon, Marty returned from the Sportsplex with what he described as a final offer. He pushed his thick main of blond hair from his forehead before continuing. He told us that if we did not move the obstacles from the tracks the OPP would certainly arrive to arrest us within 20 minutes. A small but significant modification had taken place, however, in what was demanded from us. We could retain our camp on the wye lands as long as we agreed to stay 80 feet back from the tracks. That was it! Who's trespassing? We had our answer.

RESOLUTION

No one gave the order. No one had to. Without even realizing it, we had come to a consensus from all the talk that had gone on beforehand. There was a simultaneous move towards the track. Young men and old men picked up the ties and rails that they had placed on the main CNR line. Others moved a picnic table back from the track.

Some were visibly disappointed at the outcome. The women in the Abraham camp seemed particularly let down. Said Diane, "All our lives we have been put down by officials in uniforms. They always get their way, and we always have to bow down before their power. It's hard not to see what happened here today as a continuation of the old story."

Most of the adults went home to rest and wash up. But as evening approached, the camp began to come alive again. Our boys Sam and Riley and their big gang of cousins were in particularly high spirits. They waved at the freight trains as they rolled once again through the reserve. From the west came car after car full of lumber, stripped from lands in British Columbia where the question of aboriginal title also remains unsettled. I wondered how the Aboriginal people were doing in their actions out there.

The more I looked at the injunction the more satisfied I became with the outcome. Technically we had not fully fulfilled the terms of the document. Our being allowed to retain our camp on the wye lands was a tacit admission that we were not trespassing. The CNR was in legal difficulty, and a process would have to be set in motion to deal with the unresolved issues of land title. The federal government would have to be involved on both the side of the Aboriginal people and the side of the crown corporation. What we had obtained, then, was probably more significant than a letter from Doug Lewis. A start had been made.

For Rayno, there was definitely a sense of getting even. As we returned to the camp, he pointed to a rock outcrop. "When I was a boy, we lived up there in a log cabin," he said. He continued with the story. Apparently our protest camp was on the site of a small village where CNR workers had once lived. When Rayno would play in that community, he was often treated as a trespasser. He, however, knew better. As his elders told him, the CNR workers were actually living on reserve land, even if they treated it as their own property.

In the weeks that followed, I was able to reflect on what had happened with Lena's brother Frankie. He never did return to his job at the Weldwood plywood mill in Longlac. From his role in representing Long Lake 58's position to the outside world through the media, Frankie had gained a new sense of his own potential. "I found out I can do that kind of work," he said.

POSTSCRIPT

My level of optimism has diminished substantially in the three years since the Indian summer. Unfortunately, the clarity that emerged in 1990 surrounding the basic unresolved issues of land title has since disappeared. One hears Long Lake 58 people speaking of various bureaucratic "negotiations" under way, but it seems clear these processes are partially designed to obscure federal and provincial unwillingness to deal directly with the reality that the laws of Canada are being broken as long as unceded Indian lands are being stripped of their resources without Indian consent. As far as I can see, a big part of the problem is the legal profession's exploitation of a large business opportunity that might as well be called the aboriginal rights industry. It seems that once most lawyers get hold of the basic political issues, the enlivening community dynamic gets lost in jargon and esoteric technicalities that sharply narrow the discussion to a small group of elite insiders. The larger part of the aboriginal community, whose destiny is also at stake in the closed-door processes dominated by lawyers and other assorted technocrats, is effectively cut out of the decision-making action. A malaise takes over based on misplaced faith that somehow some experts somewhere will resolve the basic conflicts. Just wait another year, another decade, another generation, the elite insiders seem to advise those not privy to the jargon of Canadian legalese or to the self-serving function of the large aboriginal affairs bureaucracy. And so the growth of the dynamic spirit of self-determination is again stunted. The old top-down pattern of hierarchical rule prevails once again. And the CNR and the Canadian government run the railways as if nothing ever happened.

NOTES

1   See Hall, "Indian Summer, Canadian Winter," *Report on the Americas*, Vol. 25, No. 3, December 1991, pp. 34-38; Geoffrey York and Loreen Pindera, *People of the Pines: The Warriors and the Legacy of Oka* (Toronto: Little, Brown, 1991).

2   See Paul Tennant, *Aboriginal People and Politics: The Indian Land Question in British Columbia, 1849-1989* (Vancouver: University of British Columbia Press, 1990).

3   Canada, *Atlas of Indian Reserves and Settlements, Canada 1971* (Ottawa: Indian and Inuit Affairs Program, Reserves and Trusts Group).

4   See Bruce W. Hodgins and Jamie Benidickson, *The Temagami Experience: Recreation, Resources, and Aboriginal Rights in the Northern Ontario Wilderness* (Toronto: University of Toronto Press, 1989).

5   See John Goddard, *Last Stand of the Lubicon Cree* (Vancouver: Douglas & McIntyre, 1991).

6   The document was distributed widely to the media in August of 1990. A copy is included in the CNR's application for an injunction to the Supreme Court of Ontario, 17 August 1990. Court file no. 53538/90.

7   Good surveys of aboriginal land disputes in Canada include Boyce Richardson, ed., *Drum Beat: Anger and Renewal in Indian Country* (Ottawa: Assembly of First Nations, 1989); Ken Coates, ed., *Aboriginal Land Claims in Canada: A Regional Perspective* (Toronto: Copp Clark Pitman, 1992).

8   Canada, *In All Fairness: A Native Claims Policy* (Ottawa: Minister of Supply and Services, 1981); Thomas Berger, *Fragile Freedoms: Human Rights and Dissent in Canada* (Toronto: Clark, Irwin and Co., 1982), pp. 219-257.

9   Canada, *Outstanding Business: A Native Claims Policy* (Ottawa: Minister of Supply and Services, 1982).

10   See Hall, "Self-Government or Self-Delusion? Brian Mulroney and Aboriginal Rights," *The Canadian Journal of Native Studies*, Vol. 6, No. 1, 1986, pp. 77-89.

11   See John S. Long, "No Basis for Argument: The Signing of Treaty Nine in Northern Ontario, 1905-1906," *Native Studies Review*, Vol. 5, No. 2, 1989.

12   Hall, "Where Justice Lies: Aboriginal Rights and Wrongs in Temagami," in Matt Bray and Ashley Thomson, eds., *Temagami: A Debate on Wilderness* (Toronto: Dundurn Press, 1990), pp. 223-253.

13   Ibid., p. 236.

14   See Hall, "What Are We? Chopped Liver? Aboriginal Affairs in the Constitutional Politics of Canada in the 1980s," in Michael D. Behiels, ed., *The Meech Lake Primer: Conflicting Views of the 1987 Constitutional Accord* (Ottawa: University of Ottawa Press, 1989), pp. 423-456.

15   *St. Catherine's Milling and Lumber Company* vs. *Regina*, in United Kingdom, *Appeal Cases before the House of Lords and the Judicial Committee of the Privy Council*, Vol. 14 (London, 1889), p. 59. See Hall, "The St. Catherine's Milling and Lumber Company versus the Queen: Indian Land Rights as a Factor in Federal-Provincial Relations in Nineteenth-Century Canada," in Kerry Abel and Jean Friesen, eds., *Aboriginal Resource Use in Canada: Historical and Legal Aspects* (Winnipeg: University of Manitoba Press, 1991), pp. 267-286.

PART THREE
Economic Development

Dressing furs at de'Medici, Nipissing First Nation.

Chapter 6

Co-management of Lands and Resources in n'Daki Menan

Mary Laronde

Since lumbermen first arrived on the boundary of n'Daki Menan in 1877, the Teme-Augama Anishnabai have been trying to enter into a treaty with the new governments that were coming into our land. Up to that time, we had lived freely and independently under our own system of laws. Our land, n'Daki Menan, was held in common by all Teme-Augama Anishnabai, and it was and is our sacred responsibility to care for our land, follow the laws of the Creation, and provide for the future of our children.

We have lived on our lands for thousands of years, following the four seasons. We followed natural laws, and the land provided everything for our people. We did not roam around following game, as is commonly thought. We lived on these lands as a distinct political unit, under laws, for probably 10,000 years, because our creation as a people happened right here on n'Daki Menan "after the great flood." We have scientifically proven 6,000 years of occupation of n'Daki Menan, and we evolved a very complex but totally natural way of managing our lands. It is this knowledge and this view of our lands as our Mother that we bring today to the efforts of co-management, or, as we prefer to call it, shared stewardship.

Sharing stewardship and the authority to 'manage' lands and resources has been part of our objective for a new kind of treaty. For us, it is a way to fulfill our sacred obligation to protect the land for future generations, yet respond to the modern world, where we as the indigenous people of our territory can be Canadian yet not have to surrender what we see as basic human rights. We do not believe that our sacred trust responsibility to our future generations cannot be acceptable to Canadian society. We know that others have come to love our land. We also know that others have come to exploit our land and destroy her ability to sustain life. The solution is a treaty of co-existence where our differences are not only accepted but used, implemented for the highest good of all, including those not yet born. Another essential part of the new treaty must be a significant portion of our homeland that will be under sole stewardship of the Teme-Augama Anishnabai. We were always self-sufficient in the past, and we need to be self-sufficient again. There will be no peace until our distinctness as a culture under our own laws is revived. And we are not talking about a reservation; we are talking about an aboriginal government that has authority over the way in which the land is used and authority to run our own affairs. We shall accommodate non-native people in our area of sole stewardship. They will have a greater say in our land management than currently exists on"public lands" under the Ontario government.

GOVERNMENT INTERFERENCE

We have 14 family territories in n'Daki Menan, and each territory has a central village site and several outpost camps. We had our seasonal rounds, and this was the way in which we managed the game on our family lands for centuries. We burned certain areas to maintain browse and produce berries. Each family was responsible for the care of its territory and had the right to its resources over others, but the land was held by all and law forbade individuals from trading or selling lands. If there were to be a division of lands and resources for evolving needs, as in granting citizenship to a new family head through marriage, it was a decision of the whole people.

These family grounds were based on geographically delineated water systems, and use was strictly enforced. In response to the new Canadian government laws, Chief Alec Paul said in 1913, as recorded by an ethnographer, that we Indians do not have to be told how to look after the game — we can look after it better than the game wardens, because we must look after it or starve. We shoot game for support, not for sport. He went on to say that we Indians have to live here all the time — we cannot kill all the game and then take the train and go 300 miles and shoot all the game there. Chief Paul also compared our system of land management to ranching: he said that the moose was our beef and the woodland caribou our sheep, the beaver our pork, and the ruffed grouse our chicken.

Despite the interference in our livelihood, the family system is still recognized and some individuals still trap portions of their original family ground.[1] But it is true that our way of life and our culture have been seriously threatened, and so has our land, and so has our existence as a people.

Our way of life was interfered with to the point where it became *illegal* for us to live as we had done for thousands of years. Even though we had not signed away any of our rights and even though the federal government acknowledged that we did not belong to any treaty surrendering our rights, the Ontario government made timber and game reserves from our lands because they were so healthy and rich, abundant with resources from which to make a dollar. When reserves were put in place, we were under the threat of arms by enforcement officers not to hunt and fish or even cut firewood for our homes. Further developments, like flooding for hydro and moving log booms, flooded people out of their homes. They lost everything and never got a cent in compensation. Until the late 1970s, government staff burned our log homes because they said that these were illegal buildings without permits.

One type of interference that almost destroyed us and from which I do not think we have recovered (but from which I believe we shall recover in years to come), was the government's policy in the 1950s that made it illegal for us to keep our children out of school between September and June. That was the time when we went to *real* school, the time that our families spent in the bush and we children were primarily with our grandparents, because our parents were always working, doing what needed to be done to live a good life. When the school system was forced on us and we no longer spent time with our grandparents, then the family system in land holdings fell further apart.

As well, a lot of our men who were in the services in World War I and particularly in the World War II found when they came home that their homes and their trapping grounds had been licensed to people who were not Teme-Augama Anishnabai. This was because more outsiders had moved into our area. So the men had their trapping grounds taken away from them in that way.

What happened on our land is that we have about 8 per cent left of the original white and red pine forest that was there. A lot of that is on the highway reserve, and along the Lake Temagami Skyline reserve, and in the area of the Wendaban Stewardship Authority. In the 1960s, the clear-cutting and the building of roads and accessing of all of the heartland of our motherland caused great concern for the elders and the people who were still using the land in a traditional way. Even though traplines were by now limited to 36 square miles, people still used the land and travelled on it a lot, and these new practices caused us great pain because it was not our way to clear the land of all of its trees.

RED SQUIRREL ROAD

Today the area around Red Squirrel Road is basically a clear-cut from Temagami to Elk Lake, except for a portion around Anima Nipissing Lake and around Lady Evelyn Lake. But in some other areas it actually is a clear-cut of that great a magnitude. Also, with these roads and the cutting, our people's trapping cabins were reached by other people and they were ransacked. Our people have lost stoves, traps, and other personal belongings. This is not something that happened a long time ago; it still happens today. I know that in Cree country it is happening all the time because access to that area has just opened up.

A few years ago, when the plans to extend the Red Squirrel Road came up, all we could say was, "enough is enough." We were confident in the whole judicial system in Canada, respectful of those laws, and expected to have the truth told and justice served. While our claim was ongoing, the governments still went ahead and were basically logging the heart out of our lands. In fact, after the cautions were put on the land, new mining was stopped and new land sales. When the land claim started gaining momentum, however, the cuts were actually accelerated. The caution did not affect timbering, because it requires only a licence. The attitude seemed to be: "Let's just cut as much as we can now."

So this cutting was all happening and we were saying, "Wait a second, we are asking the courts in Canada to declare that our title, as the indigenous people of these lands, still exists. And while that question is before the Supreme Court of Canada, or in that judicial system, then we expect fair play in that there would be some kind of agreement for any of these activities that are going on, or that they shouldn't go on." We opposed the Red Squirrel Road because it was in the only part of our territory not to have been made accessible by roads; a significant part of what was the great forest that we need for our life — and that we all need, not just the Teme-Augama Anishnabai — was being sought and would be gone in a few years, while it had taken hundreds of years to grow.

In 1988, we were in a situation where the only thing that we could do, because injunctions were not successful, was to set up a blockade at the Wendaban camp, and we blocked that road. The court decided that there was going to be a hearing, and we lost in the appeal court as well. We proceeded to the Supreme Court of Canada for a decision. On 11 November 1989, while waiting for that decision, we initiated another blockade, and it lasted one month. There were 227 arrests. Shortly afterwards, we signed a memorandum of understanding with the provincial government.

MEMORANDUM OF UNDERSTANDING

What we had been trying to do all this time, since 1877, was to enter into a treaty with the government. We had said throughout the 1980s that what we were looking for in a treaty was a way by which the government and the people whom it represented would honourably share and use our homeland with us and that we would change the present regime on our homeland to include two kinds of stewardship. In some areas, stewardship would be our sole responsibility; in the remaining areas, we would share responsibility with the people of Ontario.

The memorandum laid out three things, three processes, so to speak, but all premised on this drive finally to have an agreement. First, treaty negotiations would begin.[2] Fundamental to that was stewardship of the land and that it would be called a treaty of co-existence. This meant that we, the people of the land, would decide for ourselves how we are going to live on that land and take responsibility for those decisions. Second, because there was shared stewardship, shared jurisdiction, shared government, or shared decision-making, which we also wanted for our homeland, we also set up in this agreement a stewardship council, later known as the Wendaban Stewardship Authority. This was seen as a model for co-existence or for co-jurisdiction and sharing of decision-making on the land. The authority has 50 per cent representation from the Teme-Augama Anishnabai and 50 per cent from the province of Ontario or its appointees. The chair would be mutually acceptable to both groups. We also negotiated the terms of reference for this authority.

In these terms of reference, we were able to establish that the sustained-life principle, which explains the Anishnabai land ethic, is one of the terms by which the authority must do its planning and make its decisions. The stewardship principle of sustained life says that the land is the boss, that our decisions have to be related to the ability of that land to maintain its integrity, to be healthy, to sustain life. We must be concerned not just with human life but with all the life in that land and all the life that relies on that land to live. We call it "holisitic stewardship," where everything on the land is of value. So the Wendaban Stewardship Authority has that as one principle, and sustainable development as another. These are the fundamental principles that guide its decisions in land use.

Third, the memorandum of understanding launched a bilateral process whereby the Teme-Augama Anishnabai would examine existing timber management plans on n'Daki Menan and make recommendations to Ontario's Ministry of Natural Resources (MNR) as to how these plans should be changed. It is an interim arrangement because treaty negotiations are ongoing, and it allows for a transitional period to protect somewhat the people who rely on the forest industry for jobs and also permits these things to go on while we negotiate the treaty. It would also allow us to start implementing to some extent the kinds of stewardship that we would like to see and to do some "damage control" regarding unsustainable forestry practices.

We have a difficult problem with this kind of process because we are working within a framework in which we have absolutely no faith — namely, the timber management plans. Timber management is a very narrow way of managing the land; its primary objective, as is stated in the plans themselves, is to supply the industry.

Other issues are secondary, or, in some cases that we have seen, they are supposed to be addressed in a sort of happenstance kind of way. That is, you apply basic guidelines, and the guidelines should look after a whole lot of things, but the people are not really sure of that. This is the kind of management regime that we are working in right now.

The land bases are wrong. First, on that land mass, which is a natural biological unit, we have five different districts with which we have to deal in the plans. Within each district, for example, in the Temagami District, which is mostly all n'Daki Menan, we have two sets of plans, because the plans are made on a unit basis, and there are two units. So we are dealing with seven timber management plans. We do not agree with this kind of fragmentation of the land, because we are talking about systems — water systems, watersheds, a biological system — and no respect is paid to that. To us, stewardship does not mean merely supplying lumber.

Second, the MNR will take recommendations under advisement only and will implement them where feasible. The feasibility is determined through consultation, and the final decision rests with the ministry.

IMPLEMENTATION

Even in this limited kind of process, we have been able to do a number of things. First, we made up guidelines in the timber management plans for protection of our cultural and heritage trails, portages, campsites, village sites, and other significant places, including archaeological or spiritual ones. Second, we instituted some wetland guidelines in the Temagami District. We wanted all these wet areas to have some protection around them, because the current timber management plans ignore the wholeness of life on the land. It was our belief that as a short-term precautionary measure, these wetlands guidelines would at least provide some protection for diversity and habitat in our area.

The bilateral process has a mandate or lifespan, as does the memorandum of understanding, for three years. In the first year, we did a lot of groundwork. We sent our own people to travel these areas that were going to be cut and to get an idea of what was out there. When we put a lot of pointed questions to the technicians at MNR, or if we said something like, "What you say in your plan you're going to do and what happens in the bush are two different things — why is that?," they always said, "Our information isn't very good, it's outdated, the Forest Resource Inventory is no good," and so on. We thought that we should go and do our own evaluation and see what is out there, because this information is not available. I was told that we should not do that, because we were duplicating work and it was a waste of money. What we ended up doing was cruising and counting everything, taking everything into account, whereas the kind of cruising that the ministry was doing only took into account the timber supply. We were able to start doing such things as marking out areas that had significant regeneration, to keep those areas out of clear-cut.

In some areas of Temagami, all the pine has been taken out. What is left may be poplar or birch; now loggers are going back for poplar and birch, which is clear-cut, and inside those poplar and birch stands you could have a significant growth of red and white pine, or the higher quality, and eventually bigger trees. The new pine would be typed as poplar and birch, and clear-cut, so you would lose that 20 or 30 or 40 or 50 years of second-growth pine. Those are the kinds of things that we began seeing.

Now in the second year (1992), we are developing guidelines that we expect to be followed in timber management. In the third year, we plan to monitor the areas that have been cut, see how our recommendations have been followed, and, as well, evaluate the entire process, both in substance and in the process itself. We shall see what it is like to deal with co-management issues with the present government representatives. In a preliminary evaluation, we made recommendations that were agreed to and then ignored. We have also been told that we cannot implement wetlands guidelines or cultural heritage guidelines, or we should not try to, primarily because of the possible backlash from industry. These are scare tactics.

The other, more subtle thing that has been said to us on numerous occasions is, "We're the experts." You know, we have been through this "experts" business a lot, particularly in preparing our case before the Supreme Court of Canada. We had to have historians explain our history for us; we had to have linguists tell us and the court what kind of language we spoke; we had to have an ethnologist tell us what kind of Indians we were; and everybody argued about that, all because expert testimony was required.

Lately, we have realized that when we are dealing with issues on the land, as to the health of that land and what should be happening on that land and how to treat that land with respect, *we* are the experts. *We* deal with people who have degrees in various fields of expertise, in the present land use planning and land use system, and *we* are the experts in stewardship, because we love the land, because it is our homeland, because it is our Mother. This is the kind of ethic that is so sadly missing in present management systems.

OTHER STEWARDSHIPS
Let me give you an example of other stewardships by traditional or Anishnabai people. The Menominee in Wisconsin began cutting their

forests in 1835, when they were shunted onto that portion of what was once their great nation. They have been harvesting red and white pine, hemlock, yellow birch, oak, and sawlog material of these species since 1835. Today, they have over two million board-feet more standing timber on their lands than they had when they started cutting.

By contrast, we have virtually no red and white pine left in the Temagami forests, in the forests of n'Daki Menan. I shall tell you the extent to which this has occurred. We asked some tough questions about why the harvesting levels could continue today as they did in the past. The response was that they cannot. There is a 14 per cent shortfall of red and white pine, and a 16 per cent shortfall of the hard maple or the hardwoods, across the board for the n'Daki Menan region. It is projected that within two years, there will be a further 20 per cent reduction. We have had a very cursory look at the figures, and we think that 20 per cent is really optimistic. It is probably more like 30 per cent and perhaps as high as 40 per cent. On top of that, if the long-term sustained yield were implemented today, rather than at some other time, it would further reduce the pine by one-half and the hardwoods by two-thirds. There are no big trees between Temagami and Sault Ste. Marie. That is the situation that we are in. These are MNR's own facts. Meanwhile, logging companies are still trying to maintain the same level of harvesting.

That is in contrast to what the Menominee have been able to do on their lands. I asked Marshall Pecore, the manager there, why that is possible. He said, "because we have a policy, written by our elders and given to us in 1835. If you want to cut the trees down, we do not want to know about it. We want to be able to look out there and still see our forest. We want to see big trees, we want to see wildlife, we want to see every kind of tree that exists on that land always on that land. And we want to see trees of all different sizes, big ones, little ones. We want things to look like they are today." And they have been able to do that. And they are the experts. Notice that they are recognized as the experts in white and red pine management today. People from Forestry Canada and from MNR regularly go there to learn how to manage forests.

Here is another example in the difference in what I am saying about stewardship. When Bill Twain (his real last name is Tonene) got out of the service in World War II, he was confined by MNR to an area of land to use that had only five beaver families. It was 6 miles by 3 miles. He could barely make a living or keep fed on this land, because it had been so over-trapped by non-native people. In ten years, he had built up his beaver families in that area to 35. At that time, MNR took that property away from him because he was not killing enough beaver: according to MNR, there were too many beaver on it. He had purposely built it up so that he would have a stock there to see him through the winters. These are the kinds of things that we talk about when we talk about stewardship. We want our stewardship philosophy and principles reimplemented on n'Daki Menan.

ISSUES IN CO-MANAGEMENT
With the Wendaban Stewardship Authority in n'Daki Menan, we do have an example of how people can sit down and work together. People at the same table two years ago were on either side of that blockade. There is a dialogue; we have realized that we have a common bind or common concerns. We realize that we are human beings, that we are not the "bogyman" to one another, as so easily happens around the other issues with native rights and native management and stewardship — for example, with Algonquin Park and Oka. The process of making co-management decisions, of people sitting down and working things out together, is possible, because we have done it very well.

We need now to look at the making of actual planning decisions. It is too early to evaluate the land use decisions that the Wendaban Stewardship Authority has made; we can assess only how those decisions were made. That process, I believe, has been a tremendous success.

In another of the processes going on in the Temagami area involving the Teme-Augama Anishnabai and the other residents, we started to write a proposal for a model forest program for the whole of n'Daki Menan. Several groups — the Mid-North Forest Industry Alliance, NorthCare (which is more of an industrial-municipal advocate), NorthWatch (an environmentalist group), trappers' associations, tourist associations, ourselves and others — were able to sit down at a table and build consensus.

What I have seen developing in the group is a shared land ethic. I think that is wonderful, that people are beginning to look at the land, not just as a source of timber or a way to make money, but as something that is fundamental to our existence on this land, on the face of the Earth. The ethic is developing with all the people who reside on n'Daki Menan. I hold great hope that this will continue. People living on n'Daki Menan can co-manage the land, from what I have seen, and we can work towards the ethic that is required, which is the traditional Anishnabai ethic to manage land with deep respect and not so much to manipulate her for "products," for commodities.

Another issue about co-management with the Ontario government or MNR bears examining. When the ministry is becoming an advocate of co-management, both in process and in content (process more than content at this time, I think), the question is: "Can it?" Can that big machine, that

big bureaucracy that has total control of all Anishnabai lands and the lands
that we share with our neighbours and with the people that have come to
live here, can it divest itself of that control in our interest? It protects its
own interest in those lands. Can MNR become an agent for the public, for
the people of Ontario? Or is it always going to be in control? That is a
major issue. When you have that kind of entrenchment in both thought
and power, in processes in thinking and in how things are done, the initial
response is that the status quo must be maintained. I guess that we are
looking at systemic change — a "paradigm shift."

There are some changes taking place, but they end up being only verbal, and therefore not as significant as the words used to describe them.
For example, MNR is trying to do more about public participation, but if it
is still working in the same framework, what is going to change? That is a
large question for all people in Ontario. Can we co-manage land with the
government? We know that we can co-manage together, and the government could be our agent to implement our decisions, but can the existing
bureaucracy truly share decision-making with us? I need to stress that that
is a very crucial question.

At a recent conference at Golden Lake of the National Aboriginal
Forestry Association, everyone had stories to tell about how their traditional lands had been laid waste by the monetary interests regulated by
the provincial governments. We talked about co-management. People
were saying that we should also be asking ourselves not whether the
provincial governments are capable of it, but whether we want to co-manage with them. If they have such a bad record, why would we want to co-
manage with them? This is the sort of issue that is surfacing and becoming
focused and pointed in the Temagami area.

We have learned something significant in the last little while. When it
comes to land stewardship, the Anishnabai people are the experts. If it is
not for any other reason, then it is because we respect the perfect laws of
nature. We do not try to improve upon her, nor manipulate her for our
own selfish ends. She is what she is, and that is beautiful. I asked my elder
yesterday in Temagami if we have a word for big, mature forest, the way it
used to be around here. He said, "Yeah, there's a word, but I'll have to
think about it ... I remember that we used to always say 'anishun,' which
translates as 'really nice.'" It also says to us that it is good and beautiful.
Meegwetch.

NEGOTIATION FACT SHEET: KEY DATES
TEME-AUGAMA ANISHNABAI

1877   Chief Tonene asks to be taken into treaty to gain protection for his people from encroaching lumbermen and settlers.

1883   The federal government recognizes the omission of the Teme-Augama Anishnabai from the 1850 Robinson-Huron Treaty, arranges for annuity payments, and promises to survey a reserve.

1884   A 260-square-kilometre reserve is surveyed at the southern outlet of Lake Temagami.

1894   The federal government states the Teme-Augama Anishnabai case before a board of arbitrators: "The Dominion on behalf of the said (Temagami) Indians says that the lands are subject to the interest of the said Indians and that the Province ought to allow a reserve to be set apart, or approve of the reserve so surveyed by the Dominion upon such terms as to surrender of the Indian title in the remaining portions of the tract." Amelius Irving, counsel for Ontario, successfully argues that the case is a matter for treaty, not arbitration, and a decision is deferred.

1901   Ontario establishes the Temagami Forest Reserve.

1901   Aubry White, assistant commissioner of crown lands for Ontario, writes: "(The reserve) taking in a great portion of Lake Temagami and many million of pine timber . . . was entirely out of keeping with Indian population . . . no action was taken."

1910   The Department of Indian Affairs (DIA) asks Ontario for a reserve for the Teme-Augama Anishnabai. Ontario again cites the value of timber in its refusal.

1910   Ontario harasses the Teme-Augama Anishnabai. Chief François Whitebear writes to the Indian agent: "We have to get permission from the chief fire ranger to cut even firewood."

1911   Ontario establishes the Temagami Game and Fish Reserve and harassment escalates. The Teme-Augama Anishnabai are prohibited from hunting and fishing in the reserve.

1912   The Whitebear family settlement on Whitebear Lake is flooded by a hydroelectric development in its territory.

1921   Cross Lake is flooded also, causing loss and hardship to the Nebanegwune family.

1929   Ontario charges rent to Teme-Augama Anishnabai living on Bear Island. The DIA asks "special permission to remain without charge until . . . a reserve might be obtained."

1930   Ontario replies, saying that "as time goes on there seems to be less and less reason why lands should be set aside for the Temagami Indians."

1933   The federal government insists that "the Province has a moral as well as a legal obligation to provide these (Temagami) Indians with a reserve."

1939   Ontario again states that the area surveyed for a reserve is "too valuable from a timber point of view . . . (the Temagami Indians) should be allotted a portion of Bear Island."

1939   The Teme-Augama Anishnabai are forbidden to trap without purchasing an Ontario licence and trapping areas are reduced.

1943   The federal government purchases Bear Island from Ontario for $3,000.

1945-   The Teme-Augama continue attempts to secure the reserve surveyed in
1947   1884.

1948   The Katt (Wendaban) family settlement is flooded at Diamond Lake.

1954   Chief John Twain writes to Ontario, saying that "Bear Island is not a reserve by any means. . . We have every right to live wherever we decided to live because the Temagami Band is in the same position as before . . . we never surrendered our hunting grounds or any of our original rights to the Crown. We never signed the treaty with no government . . . all these troubles we got now will be put before the Supreme Court of Canada to definitely settle the whole matter for once and for all."

1970   Bear Island Indian Reserve Number 1 is created by an Order in Council issued by the governor-general of Canada.

1973   Chief Gary Potts files land-cautions in 110 townships within the Teme-Augama Anishnabai traditional lands and asserts Teme-Augama Anishnabai ownership.

1978   Ontario sues the Teme-Augama Anishnabai in the Supreme Court of Ontario.

1982   In June, trial proceedings commence before Justice Donald Steele for the Supreme Court of Ontario. The trial continues for 119 days over the next two years.

1983   Ontario escalates its administrative and legislative actions on the Teme-Augama Anishnabai lands. It creates the Temagami Planning Area and the Lady Evelyn-Smoothwater Provincial Park.

1984   In December, Justice Donald Steele finds against the Teme-Augama Anishnabai, saying that a chief who lived west of Temagami signed away any land rights. He also finds that the present Teme-Augama Anishnabai are descendants of the people who occupied the land in 1763.

1984   Four days after the Supreme Court of Ontario decision the Teme-Augama Anishnabai file notice of appeal.

1987   In November, the minister of Indian Affairs, William McKnight, withdraws funding of the appeal proceedings, stating that $400,000 was a "huge commitment for an appeal" and "those who have a stake in the outcome should raise the balance." The Teme-Augama Anishnabai remind McKnight of his trust responsibility and the fact that they had raised $1.6 million at the trial stage.

1988   In April, appeal hearings are scheduled for January 1989.

1988   On 17 May, the minister of Natural Resources, Vincent Kerrio, announces that construction of the Red Squirrel extension and the Pinetorch corridor will go ahead.

1988   The Teme-Augama Anishnabai Tribal Council decides at its annual assembly on 22 May to blockade any further road developments on n'Daki-Menan.

1988   In December, the Ontario Court of Appeal rules on injunctions brought forward by Ontario which sought the order of the court to remove the then six-month-old Teme-Augama Anishnabai blockade of the Red Squirrel road. In a compromise ruling, the Teme-Augama Anishnabai were ordered to remove their blockade and Ontario was ordered to stop all construction until the outstanding title issue had been addressed by the Ontario Court of Appeal.

1988   The Teme-Augama Anishnabai appeal to overturn Justice Donald Steele's 1984 decision proceeds from 9 to 27 January.

1989   On 27 February, the Ontario Court of Appeal upholds the lower court decision, denying the Teme-Augama Anishnabai's ownership of their ancestral lands with the argument that the aboriginal title had been surrendered and extinguished by any number of means. The Teme-Augama Anishnabai immediately direct legal counsel to apply for leave to appeal to the Supreme Court of Canada and reaffirm their intention to take the case to the international courts in their continuing struggle for justice.

1989   On 28 March, the Teme-Augama Anishnabai stage a one-day blockade on the Goulard logging road to serve notice to the Ontario government that the status quo and the devastation of the land by clearcut logging will not be tolerated.

1990   On 23 April, the Teme-Augama Anishnabai and the government of Ontario sign a Memorandum of Understanding to negotiate the Treaty of Co-Existence and establish a Native/non-native stewardship council over four townships in the Teme-Augama Anishnabai homeland. The Memorandum of Understanding also sets up a bi-lateral process, giving the Teme-Augama Anishnabai an advisory role in timber management on their homeland.

1991   On 23 May, the Teme-Augama Anishnabai and the Ontario government formally establish the Wendaban Stewardship Authority, a unique decision-making body with a mandate to manage four townships in the heart of Temagami's old growth.

1991   On 15 August, the Supreme Court of Canada dismisses the Teme-Augama Anishnabai's appeal, ruling that aboriginal title to their land had been extinguished when some members of the band accepted $4 treaty payments and because Bear Island had been made into a reserve in 1970. In effect, the court said the Teme-Augama Anishnabai adhered to the 1850 Robinson-Huron treaty without actually sighing it. (The Supreme Court disagreed with the Ontario Supreme Court's opinion that the Teme-Augama Anishnabai were not an organized society and therefore did not hold aboriginal title.) The court also said the "Crown" had breached its "fiduciary" obligations to the Teme-Augama Anishnabai and acknowledged that "these matters currently form the subject of negotiations between the parties."

1992   On 10 February, Chief Gary Potts announces the Vision of Co-Existence, his people's proposal for the future of n'Daki-Menan. The Vision spells out three categories of land: Teme-Augama Anishnabai stewardship lands; shared stewardship lands; and Ontario stewardship lands. In his announcement Chief Potts says: "We have had all of this land for thousands of years. We know we can co-exist on this land with our neighbours and develop structures to ensure that we are living in a framework of co-existence that provides for the pride and dignity of everyone living on our homeland."

1992   On 17 August, Bud Wildman, Ontario's Minister of Natural Resources and Minister Responsible for Native Affairs, announces his government's intention to start treaty negotiations with the Teme-Augama Anishnabai and outlines the Ontario response to the Vision of Co-Existence.

1992   On 3 September, the Teme-Augama Anishnabai and Ontario sit down at the negotiating table for treaty talks, 115 years after Chief Tonene made his first request.

NOTES

1   For a full recounting of a life lived off the land in the traditional way, see Madeline Katt Theriault's soon-to-be published book *From Moose to Moccasins*. Madeline lost everything when Diamond Lake was flooded, and now lives in North Bay.

2   *Editor's note:* On 22 October 1993, the Teme-Augama Anishnabai and Province of Ontario reached an Agreement in Principle that will lead to a treaty of co-existence. The Assembly of the Teme-Augama Anishnabai are starting the process of ratifying the Agreement in Principle as we go to press.

Chapter 7

The Fur Industry in Nipissing First Nation
Philip Goulais

The Nipissing First Nation is situated on the north shore of Lake Nipissing, just west of North Bay. Our community of Duchesnay, within the reserve of Nipissing, abuts the property that belongs to the City of North Bay. As we come further west, our neighbour to the east of us is the Town of Sturgeon Falls. Highway 17 runs through our land, about six miles north of our community. We have a land base of about 60,000 acres, taking in about 30 miles of lakefront. This is home for potentially around 1,600 members, although there are currently about 800 living within such communities as Beaucage, Duchesnay, Garden Village, Meadowside, and Yelleck.

Nipissing has been involved in the leasing of land for some time. Some local entrepreneurs within our community have been successful in business and are still doing quite well. But my focus here is on what we have done collectively in our community. As part of land-leasing, we lease land in the residential areas, as well as for commercial-industrial purposes. In our residential area, we have a subdivision known as Jocko Point: 300 lots along the shore of Lake Nipissing — 150 on the lake side of the road, and another 150 on the north side. There is another subdivision, opened in 1978, known as Beaucage, out near Beaucage Point. It was the first major community that was settled there in our history. At one time, it had a church and a school-house, and it was a well-known area where the people used to meet to talk and have ceremonies and deal with the government and the missionaries. Now there is a park, and the subdivision is just a bit west of there. This residential land-leasing generates revenue for our community.

We have industrial land, which is known as the Couchie Industrial Park, named after Ernest Couchie, one of our former chiefs who passed away a few years ago at the age of 99 years. Within that park we have Rainbow Concrete Industries, which is a major employer in our community. We also have New Venture Auto, Northern Brick and Tile, Northern Floral Distributors, and Pro-North Trucking. Of course, one of my favourites is the de'Medici Fur Plant, with which I was involved for some time.

BUILDING AN INDUSTRY

For 300 or so years, our people have been trapping furs; and for somewhat less time, we have been auctioning them. Now our community is involved in the third stage of the industry — dressing them. In fur-dressing, one takes a raw fur and prepares it to the customer's specifications, so that it is in a finished state and can be turned into garments. We hope to become involved, in the future, in the industry's fourth stage, manufacturing fur garments.

The de'Medici fur plant is international: our joint-venture partner is de'Medici of Milan, Italy, which represents 51 per cent of the joint-venture project. Our community, through the Nipissing Band Holdings and Investment Corporation, holds the remaining 49 per cent. We are currently dressing furs for government-run manufacturers in Copenhagen, in France, and in other parts of the world. We also deal with people from St. Petersburg, and Poland, and of course, we have furs from North America, too. I can say that probably the best beaver pelts that we are getting come from Northern Ontario, but we also get furs from Seattle, New York, and other places. In fur-dressing, we really do not have a lot of competition. We are not competing with manufacturers: we work for the manufacturers. Our job is to take the raw fur, process it, and prepare it properly. There are not too many fur-dressers in Canada.

This project developed from a study that we sponsored with three consultants in 1987 and with some financial support from Nipissing Band Council and from Canadore College of North Bay. The results of our study and of another earlier one in James Bay indicated that fur-dressing would probably be profitable. After we completed the study in the fall of 1987, we started to negotiate with fur-dressers in Canada (in Winnipeg, Toronto, Montreal, and Quebec) to see if we could convince them to come into our industrial land and build a fur plant that could employ our people. That is the whole driving force behind why we lease land, and why we thought of going into fur-dressing: we wanted long-term employment for our people. The revenue from land-leasing and industrial land has some value, but new jobs have been — and still are — the main issue here. We found that we had spent time and money on these negotiations in Canada to no avail, as we could not convince anybody to locate in our industrial park on Indian land. The market was down at the time, so some plants were closing down, rather than building or expanding. As a result, we put the consultant's study on the shelf.

After a couple of months, de'Medici came to us from Italy. It had learned of our project through a person who is in the fur industry and who also deals throughout the world in furs. He brought de'Medici's general manager and president into our community to meet us and talk about our proposal. They indicated that they were prepared to expand to Canada. The father endorsed the idea of joining up with the Aboriginal people here as partners. We were of course quite interested, and then we decided that, rather than just lease land, we were going to do business as a partner. These negotiations lasted until the fall of 1988.

I went over with a team to the de'Medici fur-dressing plant in Milan to find out about the company, and to determine its level of credibility. We discovered that it was world-respected. Was this proposed fur-dressing plant something that we could have in our community and keep it environmentally friendly? Would it be something that would be dangerous to the health of our people? Were there chemicals involved? Was this the place where we wanted to see our people work for a long period of time? Was this something that we really wanted? The conclusion of our own evaluation was that it was something that we felt would be good for our people.

Back home, we held some general public meetings to discuss key issues. We talked to the community about the process of fur-dressing, environmental concerns, and job creation. The community received it well: people were very interested in having the chief and council continue to try and build a fur-dressing plant at Nipissing.

On 3 February 1989, I signed an agreement with de'Medici to pursue a joint-venture business, conditional on funding from federal and provincial governments, environmental approvals, and a whole number of things. The actual homework started that day. We got busy, and we were able to secure funding from both the federal and provincial governments, from a trust company, from our band, and from de'Medici Italy; it was a five-way, cooperative arrangement that we managed to organize.

In April 1990, we sent 11 students to Italy to learn the trade as apprentices. They returned home in August for a holiday and went back to Italy until just before Christmas, in December 1990. During the same period, we had started construction of the new plant. On 29 June 1991, we officially opened it with the 11 full-time workers, and as of January 1992, we have 40 full-time employees, and we plan to increase that number.

We have furs coming in from different parts of the world, including Canada and the United States, and we have achieved now the quality level that the garment manufacturers expect. We are at 100 per cent in quality; but we are not yet at 100 per cent in productivity. That will come with experience, because some of the employees have just started recently, and we have only been truly in business since June of 1991.

CONCLUSION

Things are going quite well, and the fur industry seems to be coming back in different parts of the world; so, of course, we are happy to work for customers that have a market and are interested in providing us with work. It has been a good experience for all of us at Nipissing. We still have a number of bugs to iron out, but things are coming along.

In the last 18 years, spending 4 as deputy-chief and 14 as chief, I have seen the benefits of economic development in our community. Our people can secure full-time jobs, especially our post-secondary graduates, who have to find employment either within the First Nations or in a non-native community. When I was on the Northern Development Council about three years ago (1989), we had a study done, which showed that we lost approximately 25,000 of our youth from Northern Ontario, our educated youth, to the south. We conducted workshops throughout our own communities and the City of North Bay, and in the aboriginal groups from the north, from the James Bay area. The main reason that we found for this loss of our young people was lack of jobs here; if we can keep our jobs and our youth at home, they can make a contribution to our community, too. With our youth, with their education, combined with people with experience, we have a good future.

In my view, economic development is going to play a key role in re-establishing aboriginal self-government. I hope that in the future in the First Nations communities in Ontario, particularly in Northern Ontario, we can continue to secure more projects that will be self-sustaining, so that we can be more self-reliant in our communities. I am certainly a strong advocate of economic development, of creating employment, and I have seen the resulting economic and social improvements within our community. *Meegwetch.*

Chapter 8

Economic Development and Healing in Mississauga First Nation

Gloria Daybutch

Mississauga is a First Nation located a few miles west of Blind River. It is a small community, with only 4,887 acres and some 280 people living in the area at any given time. The Mississauga First Nation is growing in a socio-economic sense, because the community is committed to a holistic approach, where both personal health and economic well-being are important and where both affect each other in an integral way. The problem for many First Nations is that they seldom practise the holistic approach to growth. For balance, it would be most helpful if people worked a little on all aspects of growth rather than focusing on one aspect alone. Economic development is, first of all, the development of people; it is not just making money or creating jobs. If economic development in a community is not working, there is probably something lacking in other developmental areas such as emotional or spiritual growth.

Our community has a daycare centre operating out of the second floor of the fire hall, where nine people work full time, and a women's shelter or a family resource centre, with seven full-time staff. A new daycare centre is currently being constructed for 40 children, including 6 infants from 6 to 18 months. The Family Resource Centre has been in operation since 1985 and serves all women and children in abusive situations. It provides counselling and outreach services to the community's people. Staff members from the centre are now going to high schools and giving presentations on dating and violence, and date rape.

The community has five functioning and active committees that make up part of the "directing mind" of the community in terms of development and growth. The Education Committee drafted proposals to obtain an education adviser to work out of the local high school, coordinating activities with students, teachers, and parents. A research project was recently approved to develop a Native Studies component in all elementary grades and subjects, from junior kindergarten to grade eight. A Cultural Committee has held ten powwows in the past few years. A boys' drum group is starting up.

The challenge that our community and most other aboriginal communities face is to create a sense of unity within ourselves, our families, and our communities. Unity starts with the individual, by getting rid of the idea that we are torn between two worlds — traditional and non-traditional, aboriginal and non-aboriginal peoples, the past and the present. There is only one world to be in: ourselves. We must live our own truth as we understand it. For Aboriginal people, the one truth is the spirituality or Creator within us. If we find that truth, development begins from the inside and moves outwards. We have been trying so hard to develop from the outside, and we wonder why our projects keep falling apart. A lot of personal healing and healing circles are currently taking place in Mississauga First Nation — talking circles with youth are ongoing, a men's support group has started, and many couples are quitting abusive drinking and refocusing on spending time with their families.

It makes sense that economic development projects fail when people are kept on even though they are not mentally, physically, or spiritually able to work. Grandiose plans mean nothing if participants are not stable enough in their personal life to be honest, disciplined, motivated, and able to keep agreements and finish projects. Unhealthy people cannot work together because they do not trust each other. Social development is necessary for economic progress in our First Nations communities. Our people are attracted to wellness.

As a community, we need a common vision that comes from inner knowing of universal truths. There are in Mississauga unwritten but strongly felt principles and processes that define our reality. In our community, human values are considered first, before we opt for economic opportunities. We oppose development that is going to destroy the natural habitat and ways of our people. We have a strong sense of community and respect for nature and the environment. Jobs that harm the Earth or destroy community life and human health for future generations are not positive; they are anti-development. They destroy the future.

We want to be sure our people are fully consulted on hydro-electric dams and generator plants or on the possibility of a uranium refining plant operating close to our community. We do not object to industrial development per se, but economic development must be value-based and directed by the community. When we are in control, or at least in partnership, we can shape our destiny in other areas, such as the health and social aspects of our lives. Quality of life, as we know and define it in Mississauga, will not be compromised by an outsider's standard of living.

For Mississauga to prosper, we have to create a general environment that allows people to channel their own initiatives. People like to know that they can take care of themselves. There is a gas bar/restaurant/garage currently operating in Mississauga. One band member just recently purchased a portable sawmill to produce lumber for suppliers. Another member is constructing a small grocery store to service our band. The community has been setting up a substance-abuse treatment centre, a new daycare facility, and a family resources centre, and we plan to continue developing services for our people. Demand continues for these services regardless of our economic situation.

We believe that the following seven principles should guide sustainable economic development for our community, and we strive to operate consistently with them. Any project should be

1   ecologically and environmentally safe — presents no risks;
2   renewable — does not depend on resources that cannot be replaced;
3   future oriented — does not jeopardize survival of future generations;
4   human-centred — focuses on growth for people, not on money or profit;
5   health-promoting — helps people better themselves emotionally, physically, and spiritually;
6   encouraging self-reliance — moves away from dependency;
7   investing in future economic well-being — frees people to invest in community healing growth.

I believe that Mississauga has a solid foundation for future social and economic development. We as a community believe in and promote personal healing and growth. Our corporate policies on economic growth may not be defined in writing but are directed in the hearts and minds of our people. Our paths may be faint from lack of use, but our traditional ways and teachings are still here. Our ways may be silent at times, but they will never die. *Meegwetch*

PART FOUR
Social Development

Lena White, Thunder Bay

Professors and 1992 graduating class of the Native Human
Services Program at Laurentian University, with
Mary Lou Fox Radulovich, honorary degree recipient.

Chapter 9

Cultural Empowerment and Healing for Aboriginal Youth in Winnipeg

Brad McKenzie and Larry Morrissette

In 1986, the Youth Support Program was launched by the Ma Mawi Wi Chi Itata Centre, a non-mandated family and community service agency controlled and staffed by Aboriginal people in Winnipeg. The organization was an outgrowth of government reorganization of child welfare services and of political pressure from Aboriginal people for an agency to provide culturally appropriate family support services to the city's growing aboriginal population. It reintroduces troubled Aboriginal youth to their ancestral culture as a means to heal them and give them a sense of identity, and it insists on their active involvement in all phases of the program, as a model for individual and collective self-determination.

The Youth Support Program was initially developed to provide child-care services to the Family Support Program at Ma Mawi Wi Chi Itata. After two years, planning and implementation of a much more comprehensive, community-based program for Aboriginal youth began, and in 1988 it was developed as a separate and distinct program within the agency. This paper presents a case study of this second phase of its operation. Case study research has long been recognized as particularly appropriate for new, innovative programs, because it allows for more intensive study of key attributes, processes, and effects (Gans 1962, Isaac and Michael 1981, Pressman and Wildavsky 1974). Moreover, the resulting evaluation can lead to improved practice because of the attention given to both key variables and contextual issues (Gordon 1991).

The program provides continuing services to youth; however, and more important, it performs an advocacy role on social issues and develops new initiatives designed to heal and empower Aboriginal youth. We argue that the service model and implications studied here are relevant to other communities.

ABORIGINAL YOUTH AND UNDERDEVELOPMENT

It has been estimated that more than 40,000 Aboriginal people were living in Winnipeg in 1990, and if current migration patterns and natural growth rates continue these numbers will exceed 50,000 by 1996. Approximately 60 per cent of this population is under the age of 25, as compared to 40 per cent for the non-aboriginal population. Unemployment among Aboriginal youth is four times the rate for all youth. School drop-out rates for Aboriginal youth are extremely high, particularly during junior and high school years. As a result, fewer than 20 per cent complete high school. Only 15 per cent of youth not attending school are employed, and most of these are working in unstable, low-paying jobs. Particular groups of Aboriginal youth are most vulnerable. For example, young Aboriginal women are four times more likely than their non-aboriginal counterparts to become single parents and to face related social and economic "disadvantages." One out of every 24 Aboriginal children or young people is apprehended by child welfare authorities — nearly three times the rate for their non-aboriginal contemporaries. Family violence and child abuse are widespread, and the cycle is too often repeated. Seventy per cent of Aboriginal people are incarcerated at least once before the age of 24, and Aboriginal people are four times more likely than other youth to commit suicide (Ma Mawi Wi Chi Itata Centre 1988).

These indicators are not new; they reflect the symptoms of underdevelopment facing Aboriginal people which have been shaped by internal colonialism, institutional racism, and cultural disintegration (McKenzie and Hudson 1985, Ponting 1986b). And despite increased awareness of the importance of culture and self-identity, conventional services and programs have been slow to incorporate more than a token appreciation of these issues. Moreover, there is significant resistance within many agencies, particularly in a time of economic restraint, to recognizing Aboriginal people formally as a specific consumer group requiring uniquely designed and delivered services. Aboriginal youth are particularly disempowered because they are disorganized and do not have an effective mechanism to represent their own understandings of common needs, problems, and preferred solutions.

General recognition of the nature and cause of problems affecting Aboriginal people has led to proposed solutions that include aboriginal self-government and control over the institutions and services provided to Aboriginal people (McKenzie 1985, Ponting 1986a, Reeves 1986, Hamilton and Sinclair 1991). In the social services, major initiatives have focused on development of First Nations child and family services on reserves, and on evolution of Aboriginal child and family service agencies in several urban centres across Canada. The Ma Mawi Wi Chi Itata Centre, set up in 1985, in turn recognized the needs of Aboriginal youth as unique and launched the Youth Support Program as a distinct entity located within Winnipeg's inner city.

GUIDING PRINCIPLES

Members of the program staff were initially committed to a philosophy that emphasized aboriginal culture and identity as a means to youth development; however, operations and activities directed to this end have evolved over time. Two principles have guided the development of the program: young people must experience aboriginal culture and healing, and they must participate actively in all aspects of the program.

Culture and Healing

While not all Aboriginal people embrace the same philosophy of life, there are fundamental differences between the dominant Euro-Canadian society and aboriginal society. These two world-views (Hamilton and Sinclair 1991) have their roots in different perceptions of one's relationship with the universe and the Creator. Whereas Judaeo-Christian tradition emphasizes the dominant role of human life, aboriginal traditions see this form of life as the most dependent and least important. Traditional values in aboriginal cultures vary, but they include qualities such as wisdom, love, respect, bravery, humility, truth, generosity, and sharing (Hamilton and Sinclair 1991: 21). It is not the presence of these values that distinguishes aboriginal culture from the dominant society, but rather the pattern of expressing them. While the dominant society has developed conventions that allow its traditional ethical and moral values to be separated from everyday life, integration of these values to form a general lifestyle is much more apparent in traditional aboriginal society.

This is particularly evident in the expressed relationship to the Creator and the concept of "holism" as it applies to the aboriginal goal of healing. It is a central belief that each person's being is composed of three equal aspects. These are mind, body, and spirit, and all aspects are to be treated in a holistic fashion when illness or problems are identified.

It is useful to clarify the concept of culture as used in this paper and as conceptualized within the Youth Support Program. While Anderson and Frideres (1981: 49) define culture and origin as core components of one's identification as a member of an ethnic group, they regard culture as a rather general concept with limited empirical or theoretical utility. They stress the concept of ethnicity and note that ethnic groups are usually defined as having common subjective and objective attributes. Objective attributes include common cultural characteristics such as language, religion, and folkways, and possibly common physiological features, and subjective attributes include shared feelings as a group of people and self-ascription or ascription by others of aspects of their identity. Ethnic groups are often tied to minority status and can emerge or dissipate depending on the nature and intensity of external and internal pressures. Although the distinction between culture and ethnicity may have theoretical merit, we use the term "culture" in the more popularly accepted fashion in this paper and include both objective and subjective traits.

Ethnic and cultural characteristics are frequently described in order to illustrate differences among population sub-groups, but this often leads to a rather passive approach to culture. This tradition treats cultural characteristics as attributes to be encouraged and preserved only as long as they do not challenge mainstream or conventional values and practices. In social work practice, this approach leads to suggestions for modifications towards dominant modes of practice (Red Horse 1980, Hull 1982, Cross 1986), but only rarely examines culture for its potential as a source of liberation and empowerment. Anderson and Frideres's (1981: 53) discussion of types of ethnic awareness helps to clarify this distinction. At the individual level of analysis, one can differentiate ethnic awareness from consciousness. Awareness reflects knowledge of ethnic traits, which may, however, be regarded as no more meaningful than other physical or social characteristics. Ethnic consciousness, in contrast, reflects possession of ethnic traits that are of considerable importance to the individual and shape his or her self-identification. A similar distinction separates ethnic category and ethnic group. Although some people may be classified into a specific category because they possess ethnic traits, they may feel no sense of belonging or basis for meaningful social interaction. In an ethnic group, a number of people interact meaningfully on the basis of similar ethnic traits, which become the basis of a sense of consciousness and belonging.

While these distinctions are helpful, they do not fully characterize the manner in which culture is recognized and used as a method of healing within the Youth Support Program. Here aboriginal culture involves use of traditions as an active component in developing both personal and political dimensions of self-identity. Thus knowledge of traditions and of the historical treatment of these by dominant society helps develop consciousness about culture of origin and the impact of colonialism as those relate to current aboriginal realities. When viewed in this fashion, culture and cultural programming become central components of healing and active ingredients in promoting social and political change.

Active Participation

The Youth Support Program attaches priority to the participation of Aboriginal youth. This is stressed at the very beginning of any youth's involvement at the centre and in an ongoing fashion in a process that involves identification of needs and issues as well as design and implementation of solutions. In many other programs the goal of participants' input and control is articulated frequently as an essential principle in empowerment. However, most programs do not achieve a level of participation that approaches this expectation, and too often efforts aimed at developing participation remain at the tokenistic or consultative level.

The Youth Support Program initially acted on this principle through implementation of an Aboriginal Youth Needs and Planning Project. Liaison took place with existing Aboriginal youth groups and organizations, and animation activities were initiated among the general population of Aboriginal youth. Youth involvement and a needs assessment study led to identification of thirty issues, with the most important being educational problems, the need to clarify and strengthen an aboriginal identity for youth, drug and alcohol abuse, and unemployment. Youth assemblies have been organized by youth leaders, staff, and volunteers around key issues and have attracted as many as 500 youth; they are now an essential and ongoing component in planning for new programs and initiatives.

OPERATIONALIZING PRINCIPLES
The two principles highlighted above — aboriginal culture-healing and active participation — lead to an approach that is both restorative and empowering, as youth are encouraged to take not only more responsibility for their own development but also increased collective responsibility to help others and to promote political and institutional change. Traditional lodges and balanced relationships are the touchstones of this approach. First, there is strong attachment to the lodge, which at its most generic level is the centre or point from which an aboriginal nation begins to construct its social relationship with Creation. Traditional lodges, then, are central to development of an aboriginal meaning of life and key sources of aboriginal identities, and within this tradition elders serve as teachers and healers.

Second, emergence of a positive aboriginal identity involves the notion of balance. The colonization of Aboriginal people by the dominant Euro-Canadian society weakened traditional social, economic, and political systems. Land was stolen and expropriated, traditional resources were destroyed, communities and families were disrupted, and the spirit of Aboriginal people suffered as social disintegration became widespread. For too many Aboriginal youths, coping has involved substance abuse, poor educational achievement, unemployment, criminal activities, and experience with family violence both as victims and as perpetrators. Intervention with youth must involve both elimination or reduction of these destructive coping mechanisms and the restoration of balance by replacing these with a positive individual and collective identity.

Despite the impact of colonialism, some aboriginal traditions have survived; in fact, the past decade has seen renewed interest in traditional aboriginal systems and teachings. When combined with conventional knowledge and education, these traditions and teachings become instrumental in forming new, more constructive ways of coping for Aboriginal youth. Thus, the search for truth and for a response to contemporary problems and issues includes the search for balance in a new relationship with the Creator and Mother Earth. This balance reflects a commitment to sustainable development, including both tangible attributes, such as land and resources, and less tangible attributes, such as culture and traditions. The role of the traditional lodge is central in this quest, which involves learning about the meaning of traditional cultural practices and ceremonies.

Several goals guide the service model adopted by the Youth Support Program, and these stress a culturally based vision of youth empowerment. First, while healing of all aspects of one's being is central to programming, spiritual healing requires special attention, through learning about and experiencing the practices and traditions of aboriginal culture. The spiritual aspect of aboriginal identity has suffered most dramatically because of the loss of cultural consciousness, and decolonization of the individual requires special attention to this component of one's being. Second, programs for Aboriginal youth must respond to all aspects of need, including that for income and shelter. Third, cultural teaching and knowledge must be fully integrated into all program components, and traditional knowledge must be used to help organize personal and social relationships as well as political structures and processes. Fourth, programs must incorporate both personal healing and developmental objectives. However, sufficient progress in relation to healing, and support during this process are required before other objectives can be fully realized. Fifth and finally, social work services must incorporate traditional cultural teaching as a central aspect of helping. Here it is important to distinguish between the more common attitude towards culture in social work practice, which includes recognition of value differences, and the use of knowledge and practices of culture of origin as an active, empowering agent for change.

PROGRAM COMPONENTS
In the Youth Support Program, program delivery is guided by the culture-based philosophy summarized in the previous section and by the program's relationship to the community. For example, staff members interact as fully contributing members in community events and issues, including feasts and ceremonies as well as controversial social and political issues. In

addition, the program depends on exchange between staff and youth both to provide direction in service and program development and to implement new initiatives.

Use of youth assemblies as a planning and organizing tool is consistent with working with youth on issues defined as important by this and the larger aboriginal community. These assemblies, organized to educate and develop a strategic plan for follow-up action, represent a developmental approach to youth programming. Through their involvement in creating new initiatives, such as the survival school, the youth develop new knowledge and enhance their own self-esteem as they become part of a collective effort to promote change or develop more innovative institutional responses in the community.

New Directions: Healing Our Youth

Another initiative that is focused more directly on the healing of Aboriginal youth is the New Directions: Healing Our Youth Program. This intensive group-training program, set up initially in Alkali Lake, British Columbia, was "piloted" in Winnipeg with two groups of youth in the summer of 1990. The experience led to adaptations in the model, including follow-up support services after initial intensive week-long training.

Youth are referred from social agencies or self-referred as a result of peer contact with previous graduates. While attendance is voluntary, and a new group is organized approximately every five weeks, there is continuing demand for this training. Its effectiveness in reaching Aboriginal youth makes it one of the program's most important ongoing activities. Well-trained staff members are essential, as participants often raise highly emotional and sensitive issues concerning their personal lives or their relations with community institutions.

Each new training session has between 25 and 30 participants. The training emphasizes personal growth ,and issues of abuse are frequently identified and shared during the initial week of training. It incorporates traditional teaching, and the talking circle facilitates sharing and the resolution of personal issues and problems. There are also opportunities to learn about the effects of colonialism and about resources and services available to youth in the community as participants move from the individualization of problems to group understanding and collective action.

Follow-up support services are provided in two ways. First, graduates must participate in either a life-skills program or a talking circle for a minimum of five weeks. The life-skills group meets three times a week, and its primary goal is to assist participants to set personal goals and take some initial steps in realizing these. A group organized as a talking circle has an unstructured agenda, and meets twice weekly. Second, collaborative work with other agencies and services ensures that youth who require further action or support on issues such as abuse, trauma, or education receive timely assistance.

Youth have demonstrated a high commitment to the training, and in 1991 alone there were 325 graduates from the program. Many have become active in other areas, including community education to address alcohol and drug abuse and supportive efforts concerning the abuse of Aboriginal women and children. Some participants have returned as volunteers to the program and have become leaders in development of the survival school and initiation of a Bear Clan Patrol to increase community safety. Many now exercise more responsibility in choices about education and employment and work to defend individual rights when these are violated.

Other Initiatives

The development of a survival school for Aboriginal youth has been a major accomplishment. This school, incorporating culture-based educational content for youth who would prefer this option or who had dropped out of conventional schools, was initially requested at a youth assembly. A follow-up study demonstrated sufficient need, and interested youth helped to establish a detailed plan and advance the proposal through the approval stage with the school division. The new Children of the Earth School, which includes cultural programming within the required provincial school curriculum, began operation in the fall of 1991. This aboriginal-controlled school had a student population of 230 in grades 9 to 12 in its first year of operation, and it has now been expanded to serve students from kindergarten to grade 12.

Another service is the Judicial Interim Release Supervision Program. Individual and group intervention is provided to youth between the ages of 13 and 18 in conflict with the law. Through advocacy, preparation of bail plans, and post-bail supervision, Aboriginal youth are assisted to remain in the community and to assume greater responsibility for their actions. Culturally based intervention, including contact with elders and traditional ceremonies, is used as appropriate, and staff members have access other resources, including the New Directions: Healing Our Youth Program and the Children of the Earth School. Staff roles include advocacy and support, as well as social control when youths violate probation and become reinvolved in criminal activities. Experience has demonstrated that intervention must be very concrete and centred in the reality of the offender's experiences. For example, intervention pertaining to drug and alcohol problems must be based on the actual experiences of youth on the streets, not introduced artificially through abstract presentations or resources developed for other groups.

Another initiative was a response to unemployment. This involved the launching of a youth cooperative, which provided contractual services in building maintenance and cleaning and promoted responsibility and self-esteem among participants.

The most recent major initiative, sparked by a youth assembly, relates to community safety. Traditional institutions were based on the clan system, with the Bear Clan involved in administration of justice. Drawing on this tradition, a Bear Clan patrol has been developed to work within the aboriginal community in cooperation with police and other agencies. The patrol, which became fully operational in April 1992, is governed by a steering committee of 12 inner-city Aboriginal women. Members of the patrol assume roles that include protection, mediation, support, and advocacy, and they frequently intervene in situations involving family violence, solvent abuse, and prostitution. Staff and volunteers engage in street patrols and respond to requests for specific intervention, particularly in situations of domestic violence.

The components of the program summarized here do not fully capture the range of activities undertaken or the dynamic nature of interaction with the community. Additional services include direct intervention with individual youth, participation in community vigils, protests concerning the plight of women and children, and involvement in a variety of public education efforts such as conferences on racism and family violence. All programs make frequent use of sweats and ceremonies, and elders act as teachers and healers whenever appropriate. All programs combine cultural knowledge with a historical understanding of the colonization of Aboriginal people to develop a level of consciousness among youth that promotes personal growth and activism concerning community issues.

The developmental nature of this program is shown by three figures. Figure 1 illustrates common aboriginal traditional systems and roles; Figure 2 reflects the impact of colonization and he replacement of traditional systems by institutions of conventional society; and Figure 3 shows some of the recent efforts to revive aspects of aboriginal culture, traditions, and systems in responding to the needs of youth both within this program and more generally in aboriginal communities.

Figure 1.   Traditional Aboriginal Systems

Note: During pre-contract and peaceful coexistence, aboriginal societies were based on a family/clan system with respective roles and responsibilities.

Figure 2.   Aboriginal Systems and the Impact of Internal Colonialism

Note: Internal colonialism destroyed aboriginal traditional systems and roles and replaced them with systems and institutions of the dominant society.

Figure 3.   Decolonization and Reclamation of Traditional Systems

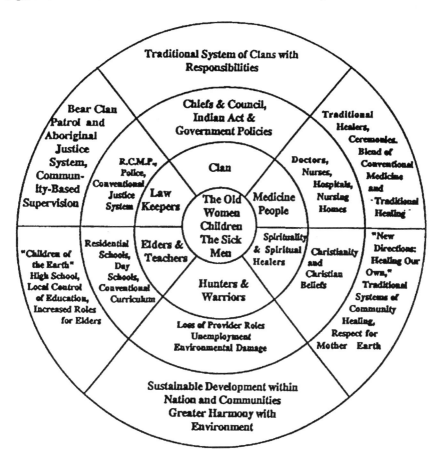

Notes: Decolonization involves replacement of conventional systems with systems that reintegrate traditional aspects destroyed during colonization.

Concepts illustrated in this model reflect the collective contributions of elders and many other Aboriginal people. Individuals acknowledged include Robert Daniels, David Blacksmith, Marilyn Fontaine, Linda Clarkson, Vern Morrissette, Wilfred Buck, and Judy Williamson.

DISCUSSION AND CONCLUSION

This case study identified a number of issues that must be anticipated and managed in developing a community-based program like the Youth Support Program. First, strategies to promote empowerment of Aboriginal youth can lead to conflict not only with conventional agencies and systems but also with aboriginal organizations and leaders who often devalue the priorities and concerns of women and children, particularly in relation to domestic violence. Thus, emergence of a critical level of consciousness can lead to efforts designed to promote more equality and social justice, both within the dominant society and within aboriginal organizations and systems. These efforts can provoke resistance and criticism both from the non-aboriginal community and from within the aboriginal community.

A second issue is that of accountability. New initiatives require new resources, and funders demand predicted and measurable outcomes. Empirical assessment of utilization rates and outcomes is possible in some aspects of these programs; it is much more difficult, however, to document the more general, qualitative effects that arise from use of cultural healing to empower adolescents or to measure the impact of social action. Moreover, there is likely to be debate about the criteria for assessing such outcomes. For example, greater self-esteem and empowerment among youth may create unanticipated problems for caregivers and institutions, as these adolescents become more conscious of their rights, needs, and wants. There is another problem concerning accountability. Effective administrative tools for monitoring service are quite difficult to design unless there is some stability in service technology and the consumer population. While these conditions may exist within selected program components such as survival school, other programs and services are much more developmental. Goals and objectives are constantly shifting in response to emerging community priorities and this makes evaluation particularly difficult. Yet this capacity to respond is one of the greatest strengths of the Youth Support Program.

Conventional bureaucracies concerned with expenditures or program standards have failed to recognize both the flexibility required in a community-based program and the value of traditional cultural practices within programs for Aboriginal youth. This failure complicates negotiations related to accountability and long-term funding, negotiations which are often time-consuming and frustrating. Success may occur because some planners and funders within conventional organizations are responsive to the philosophy and aims advanced by these initiatives or through development of widespread community support and the effective use of this source of political power. While these difficulties are recognized, it is also important to recognize that the assessment of qualitative and participatory elements can promote improvements and indicate overall impact.

Third, effective program delivery depends on staff members' knowledge and sensitivity to traditional aboriginal systems and practices and on their ability to work in partnership with youth and other people in the aboriginal community. Staff members may need to deepen their own understanding of culture and traditions and to incorporate these skills in their practice. As well, conflicting requests for service from individuals and groups in the community can be extremely difficult to mediate.

All programs at Ma Mawi Wi Chi Itata Centre are still new. Although the long-term effect of such community-based efforts cannot yet be fully assessed, the Youth Support Program has both engaged and empowered youth by incorporating aboriginal culture and traditions as a method of change. Cultural knowledge and traditions thereby become more than a means to self-identity for personal growth and change; they promote community change, including new institutional responses that reflect contemporary adaptations to traditional systems and changes within existing aboriginal organizations.

Services provided through this program are designed to replace mainstream practices and programs, and it is the experience at Ma Mawi Wi Cha Itata that incorporating culture and traditions into programs is possible, even in a large urban setting where Aboriginal people are a minority group. The benefits of this approach include those experienced directly by youth who participate in these initiatives as well as a likely reduction in future social costs which become necessary because of the long-term social consequences of colonization.

REFERENCES

Anderson, A.B., and J.S. Frideres. 1981. *Ethnicity in Canada: Theoretical perspectives.* Toronto: Butterworths.

Cross, T.L. 1986. "Drawing on cultural tradition in Indian child welfare practice." *Social Casework,* Vol. 67, 283-289.

Gans, H.J. 1962. *The urban villagers: Group and class in the life of Italian-Americans.* New York: Free Press.

Gordon, K.H. 1991. "Improving practice through illuminative evaluation." *Social Service Review,* 365-378.

Hamilton, A.C., and C.M. Sinclair. 1991. Volume 1: *The justice system and Aboriginal people* (Report of the Aboriginal Justice Inquiry of Manitoba). Winnipeg: Queen's Printer.

Hull, G.H., Jr. 1982. "Child welfare services to Native Americans." *Social Casework*, Vol. 63, 340-347.

Isaac, S., and W.B. Michael. 1981. *Handbook in research and evaluation* (2nd ed.). San Diego, Calif.: EdITS.

Ma Mawi Wi Chi Itata Centre. 1988. "Native youth needs and planning project." Unpublished report. Winnipeg: Author.

McKenzie, B. 1985. "Social work practice with Native people." In S.A. Yelaja (ed.), *An introduction to social work practice in Canada*. Scarborough, ON: Prentice-Hall, 272-288.

McKenzie, B., and P. Hudson. 1985. "Native children, child welfare, and the colonization of Native people." In K.L. Levitt and B. Wharf (eds.), *The challenge of child welfare*. Vancouver: University of British Columbia Press, 125-141.

Ponting, J.R. 1986a. "Institution-building in an Indian community: A case study of Kahnawake (Caughnawaga)." In J.R. Ponting (ed.), *Arduous journey: Canadian Indians and decolonization*. Toronto: McClelland and Stewart, 151-178.

Ponting, J.R. 1986b. "Relations between bands and the Department of Indian Affairs: A case of internal colonialism?" In J.R. Ponting (ed.), *Arduous journey: Canadian Indians and decolonization*. Toronto: McClelland and Stewart, 84-111.

Pressman, J.L., and A. Wildavsky. 1974. *Implementation*. Berkeley: University of California Press.

Red Horse, J.G. 1980. "Family structure and value orientation in American Indians." *Social Casework*, Vol. 61, 462-467.

Reeves, W.J. 1986. "Native societies: The professions as a model of self-determination for urban Natives." In J.R. Ponting (ed.), *Arduous journey: Canadian Indians and decolonization*. Toronto: McClelland and Stewart, 342-358.

Chapter 10

The KeyNorth Training Program

BACKGROUND
by Bella Brown

A t KeyNorth, we provide training for quality skills. We also give our women a sense of self-esteem, of self-worth, and a good feeling, I hope, of themselves as Aboriginal women.

I would like to offer a little bit of history about KeyNorth. It began in 1980 in Sudbury, Ontario, as the result of a discussion among local Aboriginal people at the Friendship Centre in Sudbury. They were concerned about the high unemployment rate for our Native women. People from the Friendship Centre gathered together, and in 1982 they formed a group that started KeyNorth, funded by the Canada Employment Centre. KeyNorth is incorporated, with a board of directors, and also five administrators and 20 support staff — our women, who do on-the-job training at

Bella Brown (left), coordinator at KeyNorth,
with Susan Freeland, trainee.

KeyNorth Office Services and Training

KeyNorth. We have at least four to six intakes per year. Our target at KeyNorth is women who have been out of the work-force for a long time, women who have been incarcerated, and women who have a difficult time finding and securing employment. Sometimes it is easy to get a job, but keeping it is another story. The women only have to gain skills with computers and for typing, secretarial, and receptionist work; they also have to overcome the barrier of being Aboriginal women. As an Aboriginal woman, I know that I can do the job as well as anyone else. I also know that I often have to prove myself and work harder. But that just makes me stronger.

I see that happening with our staff. Some of our women come to us with extremely low self-esteem. When I see them walk in the door, I see myself seven years ago. I think that one of the nice things about KeyNorth is that the women work at their own pace. If their typing is not up to par and someone else is typing 30 words per minute, while their typing is 10 words per minute, well, they carry on at their own rate. Instead of giving them a book and telling them to read it, showing them is a lot more helpful, I find.

At KeyNorth, we also provide opportunities to develop our self-awareness as Aboriginal women. We have workshops where the elders come and teach us about our medicines. They also teach us our role as a woman — the woman's role in the community — because years ago, the women were the organizers, while the men did the hunting and fishing.

We have resource people who come in and say to us: "This is the way to groom, this is the way to dress." Well, we know how to dress. We know how to groom. But we must know what is expected of us out there if we are going for a job interview at a non-native organization or with the government. The way I look at it, the only way to change a system is to enter the system. When we enter it, we can do something about the other issues. A lot of our women go on to higher education, and we really promote this at KeyNorth, because the better our education, the better we can speak for ourselves. We have to deal with people who are lawyers and professors, so we have to learn to speak their language. I feel that KeyNorth helps our women become stronger and think better of themselves. We bring up any issues that we feel are important, that we would like discussed, and we go over them together because we want to help each other. Every day, our women are becoming stronger.

We do internal placements at KeyNorth, and we also do placements at government offices for six to eight months. We have our support staff doing placements at band offices and at non-native organizations, where they gain more and more experience, which sometimes leads to permanent positions. We have orientation, life skills, office procedures, typing, communications, and technical skills development. We do intensive preparation for job searches. KeyNorth also operates a service bureau. We have the best prices in town, and we offer the best-quality work. If you go anywhere else, there's no way that you'll get a résumé done for six dollars a page with the beautiful fonts like we do at KeyNorth.

I was out west for five years, and I silently screamed for two or three weeks in front of the computer because I was terrified of it, and no one knew about the way I felt. I was told by one woman that the way of the future is computers, and if you want a job, you're going to have to know computers. And so, I graduated from KeyNorth about seven years ago.

Eventually, with employment equity, we hope that we can go coed, and have our young men come to KeyNorth, because we also have to think of our men out there.

I really believe in KeyNorth, and I enjoy working there. I enjoy working with the people and the board of directors. I especially like working with the support staff, because, to me, the support staff is 'me' all over again. *Meegwetch.*

CASE STUDY
by *Janet Antonioni*

Ahneen. I am a past member of the support staff of KeyNorth, and I would like to talk about how it changed my life. Before I came to KeyNorth, I felt as though I were trapped in a different type of job — child-rearing and home-making duties — which to me was like being buried. I was not getting anywhere and I wanted company. I had always given the family everything, and I felt that it was time to set out on my own ventures. For financial reasons, I needed to find employment.

What was I going to look for? Where was I going to look? Was I going to work again in a drugstore at minimum wage? I did not think that that was a great idea. My education at this point was just about obsolete. I am not going to tell you how long I was out of school — that would be getting too close to giving you my age, and I am not going to do that!

I saw an advertisement about KeyNorth, and many people had spoken to me about it and suggested that I try it. Well, I didn't get along too well with the typewriter in high school. I hated typing, I hated every minute I spent on it; I couldn't see any point in getting back into something that I had loathed all my life. After much encouragement from family and friends, I decided to investigate that area, and see if I could do it.

I went to KeyNorth to register, and I was accepted. It was not long before I was introduced to that scary old computer. This took place after many hours of struggling away on my typewriter and getting back my speed and fighting with margins and everything else. The computer is a very intimidating instrument. I know that there are a lot of people out there who are still intimidated by it, and as you get older, you find modern technology is even more intimidating. But at some point, you learn that you have to tackle it.

I looked at the monster and I said: "I'll never be able to operate that thing." But at KeyNorth, you are never alone. The participants and the staff are always there. They will try to motivate you, they will support you and assist you. There is always someone who will give you a hand when you are stuck. Needless to say, I got through Computer Introduction, went into WordPerfect, and struggled away at 4.2, only to have them upgrade the system to 5.0. I got away with it for a little while, until my supervisor found out that I was still working on 4.2. By this time, I think that I was really into the challenge. I was not going to let this idiot machine beat me. It still does sometimes but I'm persistent. I have lost many documents, made many mistakes and learned by them, and I am still battling it. I went on to learn Lotus 1-2-3. I also went on to the AES, which is a prehistoric monster and is not used very much anymore, but it was the challenge that led me to tackle it.

During my training, I was exposed to many KeyNorth programs. As my contract neared its end, I crammed. If I took too long on a lunch hour, I was taking away from what I was going to learn next. So, instead of taking an hour, I would have a 15-minute or a half-hour lunch. Then I could get back and get more lessons finished. If I spent my time having lunches, I would not get as much out of it as those who have studied intensively.

When my contract was nearly finished, I started my job search. I had sent out many applications and was called for several interviews. They were very intimidating but I was not too discouraged. I finished my contract. Three days after I left, I got a phone call that I had been accepted for a job. So I had a whole four days off between jobs. So much for holidays!

My job was a part-time position at the N'Swakamok Native Friendship Centre in Sudbury. The centre had funding for only a three-hour secretarial position with the Community Youth Support Project. I loved it! I loved having young people around, I loved the interaction. But I live 15 miles away and I was travelling to and from Sudbury to work three-hour days at minimum wage. The wage did not cover expenses. Of course, my husband was not too happy about it, and he encouraged me to look for employment elsewhere. There are not that many jobs available on the entry-level programs. There are highly qualified positions. I felt, "I have a job. It's only three hours a day, sure, but my foot's in the door and I'm not taking it out." Every year, my employers would find funding and extend my hours to a 35-hour work week for approximately six months. Then I would be back down to three hours a day — 15 hours a week. This went on for a time until they applied for funding through the Canada Employment Centre for a Native Employment Support Program. When they received the funding, I applied for the coordinator's position and got it. It is now a year and a half since we have had this program. It was all very, very exciting; there was absolutely nothing in place. I had to shop for a computer — something that I never could have imagined doing five years earlier. I found myself in a situation where I had to do it; I had to put in all my own programs and directories. That was exciting, being able to do things exactly the way I wanted them organized.

I also operate a message-taking service, because my target group is welfare recipients, and they do not have telephones. Therefore, it's very difficult for them to get their messages about interviews. So they give out my number, and I get the messages to them. I also have funding to assist them in getting to and from interviews. I assist them with their résumé-writing, and I screen and process their résumés and covering letters. I also help them prepare for job interviews, which can be extremely intimidating for them. I coordinate workshops on job-search tips and on decision-making, with facilitators from the Canada Employment Centre.

Having tackled this, I found I was brave enough to stand for nomination as a member on the Board of Directors at KeyNorth. I felt, "Who was more qualified to work in there, to represent these women, to know their issues, know their problems, know where they're coming from, know what is to be offered to them, than someone who has come from there?" I have been serving for close to two years on the board, and I enjoy it immensely. In a small way, I feel as though I'm giving a little bit back to KeyNorth and a little bit back to the native community for what they have given to me. *Meegwetch.*

Chapter 11

Reclaiming the Spirit for First Nations Self-Government

Herbert Nabigon

I looked again and saw the Indian Nations of this sacred Turtle Island. The ones put here first showed them their sacred way. They, too, were despised and desecrated by those so blind and greedy. But the sands of time run through the glass. And this time of times is nearly over. The longest and the darkest and the coldest hour of the night is the one just before the new day returns. Now is the time of hope. Now is the time to rise up. Now we must take into our hands the power of self-determination. We must stand up in our places in the sun.

I give thanks for this new day *Kitchi Meegwetch*
Art Solomon, *Songs for the People* (1990)

The New Day is returning. But what does this mean in a practical sense? As we seek to reestablish self-determination, we need to understand the past, heal the effects that this past has visited upon our people, and move back onto our path to regain our rightful place as the keepers of this land known to us as Turtle Island. Our elders are telling us now is the time, and we need to continue the process of healing that has been occurring in our communities during the last decade. In this paper, I present my ideas about self-government and how our traditional teachings about the sacred colours can help us to regain our rightful place in this land. Any understanding of First Nations self-government must review early conceptions, agreements, relationships, and treaties and current conditions. The Royal Proclamation of 1763 still stands as the Magna Carta of relations between Aboriginal peoples and Euro-Canadians in this country now known as Canada, at least for First Nations people. At the time of the Royal Proclamation, Aboriginal people held the balance of power economically, socially, politically, and militarily. The intent of the Royal Proclamation was that First Nations and the colonial government would agree to coexist in peace, and such coexistence continued until the creation of the province of Manitoba in 1870. The new province came about as a result of negotiations with Métis leader Louis Riel. Shortly thereafter, Riel was joined by Chief Poundmaker to create the province of Saskatchewan. In effect, both men were Fathers of Confederation. But history did not record their story objectively. Instead, Riel and Poundmaker were convicted of treason. Riel was hanged for his efforts, and Poundmaker was incarcerated in Stoney Mountain prison and died shortly thereafter. The balance of power shifted to Ottawa after the Riel rebellion.

Then the government of Canada began 125 years of "assimilationist" and "isolationist" policies. These initiatives have left their legacy in First Nations communities today. For example, 65 per cent of aboriginal land is located in remote areas of Canada and has very little commercial value (Ross 1987). It would be very difficult for Aboriginal people to gain some measure of self-reliance if there were nothing on their lands to develop. More land is needed, and claims are one mechanism for regaining viable land bases.

There are approximately 600 First Nations communities in Canada today. Current research on housing estimates that ten new homes need to be built in each community, and ten homes renovated, for a total of 12,000 units (Knox 1990). The government of Canada has no strategy or policy in place to deal with the housing crisis.

Unemployment also continues to be a serious problem. The rate is between 50 per cent and 90 per cent in First Nations communities. Worse still, Aboriginal people are the last to be hired in "boom" times, and first to be laid off in "bust" times. Instead, labour from other parts of Canada is imported to work in communities near First Nations, particularly in Northern Ontario, and jobs are seasonal at the best of times (Ross 1987).

> Infant mortality rates, while improving for Indian children, still remain well above the national average. This is attributed to respiratory ailments and infectious or parasitic diseases, reflecting poor housing, lack of sewage disposal and potable water, as well as poorer access to medical facilities (Ross 1987: 44).

The most disturbing statistic is the number of youth suicides:

> In Canada, there are about 19 suicides per one hundred thousand (100,000) in the age group fifteen (15) to twenty-four (24). In the same age group, there are one-hundred and thirty (130) per one hundred thousand (100,000) in the Indian population (Ross 1987: 45).

One can infer from this disturbing picture that poverty leaves deep emotional scars on people. The people act out their pain through domestic violence. Social pathologies, such as alcoholism and family violence, are well documented in publications and research reports, and solutions have been proposed by First Nations and other, like-minded people. A case in point is the Ontario government's decision of 6 August 1992 to recognize First Nations as domestic nations. This was and is a major and symbolic move by the government of Ontario.

A STRATEGY TO IMPLEMENT SELF-GOVERNMENT

To ensure that social and economic institutions of First Nations government are respected, the federal government should consider the following framework as a means of establishing a formal relationship with First Nations:

- It should be recognized that a "national will" is required to outline a division of powers. Powers will be negotiated between the federal government and First Nations. A bilateral process will be established at the appropriate time, to arrive at or include an agreement.
- First Nations should participate in the ongoing process of constitutional amendment and revision.
- Outstanding land claims should be settled, and mechanisms developed to ensure enforcement of land claims settlements. History has proven that Ottawa suffers from severe amnesia in regard to such settlements.
- Economic development should be furthered so as to reduce poverty.
- Essential social services of reasonable quality should be available to all Status Indians.
- First Nations should be able to generate tax revenues that will improve services to the people and promote self-reliance. In the long term, such taxation will reduce dependence on federal funding.
- Individual rights should be protected and respected within the context of respect for the collective rights of First Nations.
- There should be equal opportunity for all Status Indians.

The United States regards First Nations communities as domestically sovereign. Perhaps First Nations and Canada could consider the American experience and adopt a view similar to that laid out by Kickingbird et al (1977: 8):

The law is clear, however, that an Indian nation possesses all the inherent powers of any sovereign government except as those powers may have been qualified or limited by treaties, agreements, or specific acts of Congress. Therefore, while tribes have lost some of their "sticks in the bundle" they retain all the rest. So they can and do exercise many sovereign powers.

Included among those inherent powers of Indian government are the following:

1) The power to determine the form of government.
2) The power to define conditions for membership in the nation.
3) The power to administer justice and enforce laws.
4) The power to tax.
5) The power to regulate domestic relations of its members.
6) The power to regulate property use....
   Associated with this power to determine the form of government are the following rights:
(a) The right to pass laws, interpret laws, and administer justice.
(b) The right to define powers and duties of government officers.
(c) The right to determine whether acts done in the name of government are authoritative.
(d) The right to define the manner in which governmental officers are to be selected and removed.

A FOUNDATION FOR SELF-DETERMINATION
Aboriginal rights in Canada are founded on three legal bases: the Royal Proclamation of 1763, international law, and common law. The Royal Proclamation has been regulated to "historical expression of common law, rather than a source in itself of legal rights" (Platiel 1992). Judicial definition of aboriginal rights is also weak and fragile. The courts require proof of traditional occupancy and of specific land use prior to European colonization. Because the courts have not been friendly towards aboriginal rights, the best option for First Nations is to arrive at negotiated political settlement for self-government, instead of depending on the courts. First Nations must demand full and sovereign ownership of the land and resources and cultural rights, as well as legal recognition of customary law and the inherent right to self-government.

First Nations political leaders have long spoken eloquently of the need for non-native governments to recognize aboriginal right to self-determination. Yet not very often does one hear from the elders. This is strange, because the absence of balanced words of the elders lends credence to the accusation that First Nations are merely trying to "grab a piece of the pie." What is not clearly understood, even by many Aboriginal people, is that the foundation upon which self-determination must be recreated is spiritual. Aboriginal rights stem not from laws, institutions, or ideas established by governments, but from the Creator. Until this is clearly understood and accepted by non-natives, the recognition of aboriginal rights will remain enigmatic. The land and our ways of life are gifts from the Creator; noone can take them away. They cannot be ignored, explained away, or forgotten, but the gifts themselves remain eternal. Among those gifts are the four sacred directions. These directions, these gifts, are used to search for harmony and peace from within. If adopted, the four sacred directions will provide guidance to First Nations institutions as we seek to recreate our traditional forms of government which are essential in the fight for recognition.

The role of the elders is to provide spiritual direction, while the role of our political leaders is to pay attention to the people. The political leaders attempt to translate traditional teachings and values to non-native government officials. Many still recall the words of Ovide Mercredi when he was elected grand chief of the Assembly of First Nations in the summer of 1991. In his acceptance speech, he mentioned that he would listen closely to the elders and be guided by their insights and advice; elders are considered to be the foundation of leadership.

THE CULTURAL PARADIGM
The 1991 Census gives Canada's aboriginal population as 1,002,675, with 11 language families and 53 distinct languages (each with its own set of dialects) across Canada. The cultural, social, economic, political, and geographic land base of Aboriginal people has been adversely affected by intrusive, prescriptive, and burdensome governmental policies. The result is that aboriginal communities have suffered under policies that are often hostile and are designed to eradicate their cultures and languages. In response to these conditions, Aboriginal people practise unique life-styles that may be viewed as existing along a continuum. Their communities may be traditional, transitional, or contemporary/adaptive. Several belief systems, cultural practices, and traditions may exist relatively intact in the traditional setting. However, cultural revitalization may be occurring in the contemporary/adaptive community .

As a cultural paradigm, aboriginal belief systems can contribute a unique perspective for understanding the values, attitudes, and perceptions of an aboriginal world-view. The guiding philosophy of our approach acknowledges and reflects the world-view of one of the prevailing aboriginal belief systems. This world-view interprets community relations in ways that are consistent with aboriginal realities rather than with non-aboriginal interpretations of them. The following description articulates an aboriginal world-view on community. The spiritual interpretation of this world-view is divided into the four sacred directions, which are used to search for harmony and peace within (see figure 1).

East

It is believed that the Creator began life in the east, in the spring, symbolized by the colour red. Aboriginal people see themselves as having been represented first in the east. The Creator bestowed the gifts of food, feelings and vision to the People. The east wind breathes new life into our Mother, the Earth. Red is the symbol of renewal. The spring teaches us to be grateful for life. In the spring, animals have their young, and animals are both teachers and food-gifts for us. There is a strong relationship between food and feelings. Good food brings us good feelings. When we feel good about ourselves, we enjoy vision. The opposite of good feelings is inferior feelings. Today many of my people feel inferior, and strong anger emanates from this sense of inferiority. Anger from the east can be translated into many of the domestic problems discussed earlier in this paper. Traditional teachings from the east bring a message of peace and harmony into our communities. To neglect this basic truth while striving to recreate a sense of self-determination would be like trying to build a house without laying a strong foundation.

South

Yellow is the symbol of summer, time, relationship, and sun. At midday, the sun is facing south. The heat of summertime teaches us patience. Self-development is regarded as being very important for the young. Yellow helps us to understand self through family, extended family, friends, and community. It takes time to understand our identity as human beings. We learn and understand self by interacting with peers, and values are transmitted through parents. In modern times, being young can be extremely difficult for young Aboriginal people because of the bicultural context in which they live. Puberty is a time of change for all young people. Adolescence is a time of crisis. For the young Aboriginal person, it is a time to redefine one's Nativeness. The process of redefining one's cultural heritage takes precedence over all other activities, including "formal" education. Is it any wonder that their school marks tend to decline when

Figure 1.   Medicine Wheel

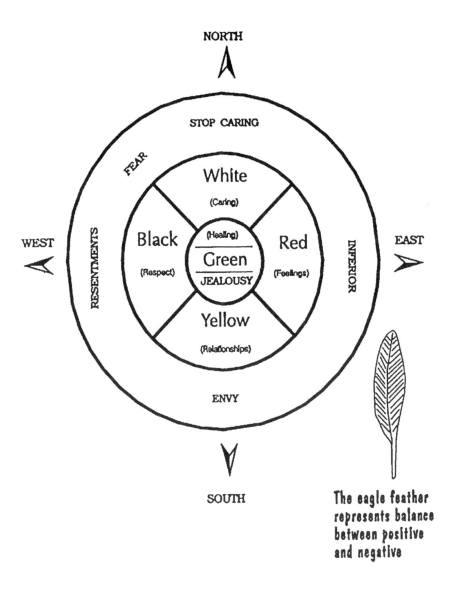

The eagle feather represents balance between positive and negative

Source: Schuyler Webster and Herb Nabigon, "First Nations Empowerment in Community Based Research," in Paul Axelrod and Paul Anisef (eds.), *Transitions, Schooling and Employment in Canada* (Toronto: Thompson Publications, 1992), p. 163.

young Aboriginal people are immersed in systems of education that impose dominant values and world-views? Often educators and parents alike forget to take this factor into consideration when there is a crisis at school. Elders and traditional teachers can help to understand and defuse the crisis. These young people are our next generation of leaders, and a return to traditional pathways and visions, supported and encouraged in the community, is an essential part of laying the spiritual foundation for self-determination.

West
Black is the symbol of fall, respect, reason, and water. Our bodies are made up largely of water and this connects us to the lakes. Water helps us to see more clearly. Respect means looking twice at everything that we do. The reality of our inner life is enhanced when we understand and implement the word "respect." Many adolescents have a difficult time reviewing their inner lives because of change and crisis. Aboriginal spiritual leaders have an intimate and intuitive understanding of adolescence and are able to provide healing to these young people. There are times when dysfunctional families overburden their older children with the responsibilities of taking care of younger siblings. This practice creates inner hostilities and resentments. The feelings of resentment destroy any self-respect that a person may have. Ultimately, how can we as First Nations expect to govern ourselves as Nations when we are still struggling to regain control of our own families? We need to regain our balance so that our communities can move forward, based on a strong foundation of respect and reason.

North
White is the symbol of winter, caring, movement, and air. It is a colour that symbolizes peace. In the winter, the Earth rests and the animals sleep. Caring can be defined by our level of interaction within family, school, community, and nation. Isolation usually indicates that problems exist, and they need to be dealt with accordingly. An action plan needs to be devised, outlining caring behaviour, which is intended to defuse isolation and the feeling of not caring about responsibilities and self. Aboriginal elders and traditional teachers understand the sacred nature of caring and its implications. They can observe how we interact and behave towards each other and, when requested, can mobilize appropriate levels of intervention. Again, without this crucial element of caring, the foundation for self-determination remains weak.

Green

Green is a healing colour that symbolizes Mother Earth. Green is also a symbol of balance and listening. The earth nurtures all the colours and living things. Spiritual leaders emphasize the importance of listening and paying attention to the dark side of life. The dark side of life can be defined by five little rascals: inferiority, envy, resentments, not caring, and jealousy. It means that we stop listening. Listening helps people make the appropriate changes from negative to positive behaviour. Listening is an essential component in the foundation on which to reclaim and recreate self-determination.

Finally, the spiritual teachings of honesty and kindness permeate all of the five colours. Honesty and kindness are the elements of the prevailing belief system which forms the core of a foundation on which to build our concept of self-determination. It is the important first step, in which traditional elders play a vital role in helping us understand self-determination at the community, as well as the national, level.

CONCLUSION

How does this foundation established by the colours relate to the "nuts and bolts" of recreating our concept of self-determination? In the last few years, elders and chiefs have stared to promote community-based healing, using traditional ceremonies, as a way for communities to start taking over their own responsibilities in the areas that each determines are important. Healing, based on our traditions, builds stronger individuals, families, and communities so that the existing high levels of social problems can be decreased and new forms of social, economic, and political development can occur without the federal government control. By its very definition, self-government is community-driven, whereby each community decides for itself the level of self-government it requires. The transition from colonization to nationhood will take time. But only if the spiritual foundation is strengthened and maintained can nationhood be realized in the manner in which it was given, as a gift from the Creator.

REFERENCES

Chiefs of Ontario. 1991. *Signing the Statement of Political Relationship*. Indian Associations Coordinating Committee of Ontario.

Frontiers Foundation/Operation Beaver. *Kanata Kapers*. Winter Garden Theatre, Toronto, Ontario, May 3, 1992.

Kickingbird, Kirke et al. 1977. *Indian Sovereignty*. Washington, DC: Institute for the Development of Indian Law.

Knox, R.H. 1980. *Indian Conditions: A Survey*. Ottawa: Department of Indian Affairs and Northern Development.

Platiel, Rudy. 1992. "Canada Reconsidered: Aboriginal Rights." *Globe and Mail*, 11 January, A6.

Ponting, Roger, and Anthony Gibbons. 1980. *Out of Irrelevance*. Toronto: Butterworth.

Ross, Heather. 1987. *First Nations Self-Government*. Background Report. Prepared for the Social Assistance Review Committee, Toronto, Ontario.

Solomon, Arthur. 1990. *Songs for the People: Teachings on the Natural Way: Poems and Essays of Arthur Solomon*. Edited by Michael Posluns. Toronto: NC Press.

Statistics Canada. 1991. *Census of Canada*.

Chapter 12

Closing Words to the Conference

Arthur Solomon, Elder

W e listened to three women yesterday. What they said tells me that spiritual rebirth is happening; spiritual rebirth is absolutely essential. The imperative for us now, as Native people, is to heal our communities and heal our nations, because we are the final teachers in this sacred land. We have to teach how to live in harmony with each other and with the whole creation. People will have to put down their greed and their arrogance before they can hear what we are saying. I am not sure that many of them will do that.

The spiritual rebirth is obvious from the conference itself. There is a whole happening going on, and more and more people are coming to events and hearing what we have to say.

I have been particularly concerned that I should help the women to heal themselves. All that I can do is to help them, which I have been doing now for thirty-some years. The women are the people who will pick up their medicine and heal the sick and troubled world. That's the way it was said by a young woman in Fredericton three years ago. But many women do not realize that they **are** the medicine. They are the centre of the circle of life for all human families. That is the place the Creator gave to them.

So we are in the process of healing ourselves, healing our communities, and healing our nations. Healing ourselves and healing our communities seem to be the hardest part, because of the violence against women. There is no way that such violence should ever be, because that is the last step down. When we are abusing our women and our children, we can't go down any further. We can only go up from here.

People like Gloria Daybutch, Janet Antonioni, and Leona Nahwegahbow were saying things that were "right on." Gloria spoke of the actual process of healing that needs to happen. Her community has created a site for the women to go to, because they were being abused. The men also said that they needed some teaching. That is the process that we have to go through. Janet spoke of training the young women to do other important things. She spoke of role models and of struggles and successes. It is obvious that the spirit people are helping us with what we're doing.

One of the realities, too, is that Native people have their spiritual and cultural ways within the prison system.

It is five hundred years now since the Europeans came; we have had a lot of patience with this society that was lost when it came and is still lost. We, the Native people, know how we got into the mess that we are in; and just as sure as we know that, we also know our way back out. That is, in essence, through healing ourselves and healing our communities and healing our nations. That process is happening, and it's coming faster all the time. People are asking all over, "Come on up and help us to see the way ahead."

There is no question in my mind that the spiritual revival is happening. It is the business of people accepting people that is the key to it all, not for what their position is but simply people accepting people. It takes time, but it's happening now, and things are moving faster than I have ever seen.

This was an excellent meeting. It is beautiful to see after all these many years of struggle. *Gitchi-meegwetch.*

Long Lake 58 blockade.